Shawnee Books

Also in this series

A Nickel's Worth of Skim Milk
A Boy's View of the Great Depression
Robert J. Hastings

A Penny's Worth of Minced Ham
Another Look at the Great Depression
Robert J. Hastings

Fishing Southern Illinois
Art Reid

Foothold on a Hillside
Memories of a Southern Illinoisan
Charless Caraway

The Music Came First
The Memories of Theodore Paschedag
Theodore Paschedag and Thomas J. Hatton

Vernacular Architecture in Southern Illinois
The Ethnic Heritage
John M. Coggeshall and Jo Anne Nast

The Next New Madrid Earthquake
A Survival Guide for the Midwest
William Atkinson

Heartland Blacksmiths

Conversations at the Forge

Richard Reichelt
Photographs by Richard Wilbers
& Richard Reichelt

Southern Illinois University Press
Carbondale and Edwardsville

Photograph Credits:
Photographs, pp. 2, 24, 42, 60, 104, 124, 142, 164, by Richard
Reichelt; p. 117, by Donald Asbee; p. 149, by Anita Worley.
All other photographs by Richard Wilbers.

Library of Congress Cataloging-in-Publication Data
Reichelt, Richard, 1945–
    Heartland blacksmiths.

    (Shawnee books)
    1. Blacksmiths—Missouri—Saint Louis Region—
Inverviews.   2. Blacksmiths—Illinois—Carbondale
Region—Interviews.   I. Title.
TT220.R45   1988   682′.092′2   [B]   88-4482
ISBN 0-8093-1475-4
ISBN 0-8093-1476-2 (pbk.)

The paper used in this publication meets the minimum requirements of American National Standard for
Information Sciences—Permanence of Paper for Printed Library Materials, ANSI Z39.48-1984.   ∞™

Contents

Preface

Several years ago my friend Tom Gipe was attending a conference of the Artist-Blacksmiths' Association of North America. Several hundred blacksmiths plus many curious spectators were attending. A young woman went up to Tom and asked, "What are these blacksmiths doing? Blacksmiths just shoe horses, don't they?" Tom replied, "Not necessarily. You don't see any horses around here, do you?" He went on to explain that while some blacksmiths still do shoe horses, contemporary blacksmiths also make a variety of tools, craft items, and art objects.

Blacksmithing simply refers to hammering hot iron. It is the most basic metals process. Since the Iron Age began, blacksmiths have translated iron into useful objects. Blacksmiths were the primary metalworkers in most societies, fabricating and maintaining almost everything made of iron. In the ancient pantheons, the blacksmith gods, the Greek Hephaestus and the Roman Vulcan, represented all the crafts because blacksmiths made the tools for all the other craftspeople. Later in human history, blacksmiths did the horseshoeing because they had the metalworking skills and equipment needed to fabricate iron horseshoes. They also made tools, iron wagon tires and wagon fittings, door hinges, fireplace cranes, roasting forks and ladles for the kitchen, boot scrapers, delicate pipe tongs that smokers used to pick up glowing fireplace coals with which to light their tobacco, and on and on. The world was full of hand-forged products and the world was full of blacksmiths. Everybody knew at least one blacksmith, and everybody from the king to the simple farmer was dependent upon the smiths. The smoke of the blacksmith's forge drifted through the air, and the ring of the anvil was heard before dawn and late at night in almost every city and town for thousands of years. We are still in the Iron Age: most of the things around us have been made with high carbon steel. The Bronze Age was certainly a progressive step, but making steel tools afforded humankind its most basic release from primitive existence.

Since the Industrial Revolution, however, blacksmiths have been displaced by machines. In fact, this "endangered species" had come precariously close to extinction in modern culture as recently as fifteen or twenty years ago. At that time a renascence began in blacksmithing that is continuing and gaining strength today. My wish to document this recent phenomenon in individual terms led to my compiling the present collection of interviews and photographs. I want to introduce a representative sample of blacksmiths to the general reader and to describe techniques and offer tips that may advance the work of my fellow smiths.

My position as a graduate student at Southern Illinois University, Carbondale, afforded me the support and time to undertake this project, and the St. Louis-Carbondale area offered me a particularly large and diverse group of working blacksmiths. The SIU campuses at Carbondale and Edwardsville have been recognized as centers of American blacksmithing for many years. The metals program at SIU, Carbondale, under the leadership of Brent Kington, has gained an international reputation for excellence and offers the only master of fine arts degree in blacksmithing in the United States. SIU, Edwardsville, has a program developed primarily by Tom Gipe, who has provided an opportunity to learn smithing for many students around the St. Louis area. Both programs have sponsored exciting, informative workshops and shows of ironwork over the years.

The smiths whom I chose to interview are representative

of various specializations and skill levels in the craft. I did not contact all the smiths in the St. Louis-Carbondale area—such would be beyond the scope of one volume—and I am sure there are many excellent subjects whom I did not include. The interviewing and photography—the latter done by myself and Rick Wilbers— were started during the fall of 1984 and were completed during the fall of 1987. In ordering the chapters, I decided to present the blacksmiths according to their approximate time spent practicing the craft professionally in an attempt to give a historical perspective and a sense of continuity.

I first watched a blacksmith work when I was five or six years old, and it made a deep impression. By the time I was ten, I had built a small forge and was hammering hot iron. Frank Turley led me into his shop in Santa Fe in 1971; I was twenty-five years old and felt further drawn to the fire and anvil. Today it remains a fascination. Blacksmithing connects me to the past, present, and future. It connects me to others and to the earth I live on. It is one of many paths.

*R*udolph Williams

Rudolph Williams is a horseshoer, general
blacksmith, and toolsmith, who has run his own
business for forty-nine years. This interview took place
at his shop in Overland, Missouri.

Rick: Where did you learn your trade?
Rudy: Well, I learned my trade in a railroad town,
Crocker, Missouri. That was back in the days
when there wasn't any automobiles. My dad was a
blacksmith for fifty years. I started when I was just
a little boy. When I was about ten years old, my
dad made me a box to stand on high enough to
reach the anvil, and he had me turn the horseshoe
corks. I knew then I was going to be a blacksmith.
It was a happy life growing up. We was all poor
but we was happy. Everybody worked, and it
seemed like everybody in the shop, even all the
horseshoers, was happy. They didn't come mad of
a morning.
Rick: About how many people were working in that
shop?
Rudy: Well, there was three to four, besides my dad.
Those days, there was no hurry. When they went
to the shop, they'd talk, but then they'd go ahead
and work.
Rick: How did you first learn your trade?
Rudy: When I was twelve years old, my dad took a good
ol' gentle horse and gave me a shoeing box and
said, "Son, this horse won't move. He's good and

gentle. You shoe him, and when you get him done, come up and tell me. Don't call me down, for you know what to do." Well, that was a happy time. I thought, Dad knows I'm gonna make it. And I did, too. When I got the horse shod, I went up there and said, "Dad, come look him over." Dad went down and picked up all the feet, looked at them to see how high the nails was, if they was clinched good. And he went back up and said, "Boys, not because it's my boy, but he's gonna make one of the best horseshoers that you ever did see." That thrilled me to death.

Rick: But why did you become a blacksmith? It's such hard work. You've got to stay in the shop when it's hot and when it's cold, and breathe the smoke and take risks with getting hurt.

Rudy: Well, when I was a little boy, I thought so much of my dad. Once I was down at my grandpa's—I was about six or seven years old—and my dad had had some pictures taken of him in the shop which I'd never seen. Grandma had this one, and when I saw my dad in that picture, I just got a feeling that I was gonna follow him. I'd dream about the shop, dream about me a-shoein' horses or fittin' shoes. I saw that from a little boy up, and I could see the sparks flying from the anvil. When I started in school, Dad and Mom drove me, but my mind wasn't on school. I'd sit there and hear the anvils over at the shop, and my lessons were gone: my mind was in the shop. Well, I kept on till I got fed up. I came very near telling my folks then, but I got through the first year of high school, and when school was out, I worked every day in the shop.

Rick: How old were you?

Rudy: I was seventeen. You see, Dad didn't have much education—eighth grade—but he always wanted me to finish high school. Mom did, too. So when I got out of the first year of high school, I said, "Hey, Dad, I want to tell you and Mom something. I love you, but I'm not going to school. I'm gonna run away from home." They knew where my mind was.

So Dad said, "Well, you know, I'll get you." I said, "I know you will but I'll keep you busy, huntin' me." When school did start, he said, "Are you going to school?" "No, like I told you, Dad, I'm going with you to the shop." Then he said to me, "You get your overalls on and your blue shirt." That's what we wore in the shop. And he said to Mom, "Don't worry, I'll get him back in school." It seemed like Dad was trying to kill me that day—just one horse after another. And afterwards he told Mom, "Well, he was singing along, whistling along—he acted like that's the biggest day he ever had. I don't know if I can get him back in school or not." The next morning he said, "You're going to school today, I guess." "No," I said, "I'm going with you." And that was it.

I've been at it forty-nine years. I've got a good business and good customers that's been with me for years. And I've been happy. But I feel kind of sorry for the young generation about learning blacksmithing. Back in those days, from a little boy right on up, I—

Rick: You had your dad.

Rudy: I sat there before I was big enough to shoe a horse and watch them at horseshoeing time. I'd see what they'd do to that horseshoe after they'd fit it, how they'd go in to open it up on the horn or close it down, drive the nails. Then I'd go home and that night I'd just see the nails going right up in there.

Rick: So you had it all pictured in your mind before you ever picked up the hammer.

Rudy: Yeah. Then when Dad made me a box for the anvil, first I started just turning the corks, and the first corks I turned up there, he didn't even have to tell me, "Good job, son," 'cause it was so much a part of me I knew every lick of it. I learned to hit that anvil, too. I had a good forge, good anvil. It'd ring like a bell. I'd know it if all the other anvils were ringing. If Dad or someone was using that one, I could tell. I went to bed many a night hearing that thing a-ringin'. It had one of the prettiest tunes to it. I never had heard an anvil sound like it before—or since then neither. It weighed about 150 pounds. I don't like too big an anvil, but 150 pounds is a nice size. I don't hit it much anymore, but I used to. They could always tell who was to the anvil.

Rick: Was your dad a good teacher?

Rudy: Yeah. He explained everything in the world to me about the shop. But one thing—you'd better put the tools back where you got 'em. If you used a wrench or a hammer or a pair of tongs, it'd better go right back where he kept it, because my dad could go in that shop the darkest night there was and pick up any tool he'd want. And he always told me, "Rudolph, listen, whatever you do, you say it's yours. If you shoe a horse and a nail come up about a half an inch, would you leave it there? No, you'd pull it out and put it up higher. If one didn't clinch good, would you leave it? No, you'd take that cutter and bend that down in a minute." So he said, "Whatever you do, say it's yours."

Rick: Claim your work, be proud of your work.

Rudy: Yeah. And that's the way I am about sharpening these moil points [jackhammer points]. If I see a

little crack in one, I take and cut it out even if I have to do it again. It's kind of hard, but Dad preached that to me, and all the time I was listening.

I had a dollar watch and I kept it on my forge. Dad gave me the best forge in the shop. And I put that ol' watch up there. And this horse would come in to be shod. I'd look at that watch and in fifteen minutes I'd have him shod. Fifteen, if he wasn't mean. I used to shoe all the way from fourteen to sixteen or seventeen horses a day. But I didn't fit the shoes. In those days we had shoes fit up by the hundreds, all over the shop. Horse come in and you didn't have to measure his foot. When we looked at that foot, we knew what size it'd take and how much time, too. Most of our shoeing was 2s, 3s, and 4s. We had a few 5s and 6s, not many. But this hot shoeing is all right. I wouldn't say nothing against it.

When I was sixteen years old, I got a dollar a day in the shop. Dad gave me a dollar a day. Of course horseshoers those days only made two dollars a day. That was good wages.

And the horseshoers, the tall ones, I've seen where they'd go to the anvil to close a shoe or open it up and they couldn't straighten up. The only time they straightened up was when they quit work, and then it took them some time to straighten up. But, me, I can shoe a horse standing up behind it.

Rick: What was it like to be a blacksmith before the days of the automobile?

Rudy: Well, there was three blacksmith shops in Crocker. And this little town wasn't over seven or eight hundred population. You'd hear them ol' anvils early in the morning and late at night. They never

did quit ringing. All day long—even after the sun was down. Horses tied all around the shop. Hitchin' racks were full, and everybody scared to death they wasn't going to get their horses shod that day. There were lots of horses, haulin' ties, haulin' wheat. We had livery barns in those days. We had two and they'd keep all kinds of buggies and hacks. One fella had thirty horses, and the other guy had forty—he had twenty teams. So there was seventy horses besides all the horses in town.

In those days, the salesmen would come to a railroad town. They'd bring whatever they had to sell—the shoes, dress goods, and all—in trunks. Then they'd get a team, and they'd go to the other towns that didn't have a railroad. Wherever you looked, you could see a horse and wagon, buggies and all. And up on main street you didn't see no automobiles but some of the finest riding horses you ever laid your eyes on. Pretty bridles with red tassles on them. And those surreys had fringe all around them. Women with long dresses down to their ankles. Lots of pretty girls.

Rick: So you were busy all the time with the horse-shoeing?

Rudy: Yeah, I didn't do nothing else. I shoed in the winter time, too. Oh boy, was we busy then. Back in those days, winter time wasn't no slow time, unless you got awful bad weather. I didn't even sharpen any plows. It wasn't because I didn't know how to do it, but that horseshoeing—that was it, you know.

Rick: Could you tell me a little more about horse-shoeing?

Rudy: Back in those days you could see the boys had pride in their horses. Take with a little colt. When

a colt was born, the farmer's kids loved that colt
so much, they'd rub it, they'd pick up its feet. And
when it got old enough to be shoed, we didn't
have no trouble shoeing it. But those that didn't
have any attention when they was young, some of
them was mean. After the automobiles came in, the
boys and young men lost all interest in the stock at
home. That's when they got bad.

And the cattlemen, they'd go out west and buy
up wild westerns that never had a halter or bridle
on. Their eyes bugged out. And they'd bring 'em in
and put 'em in the stockyard. And then on Saturdays, the farmers would come and climb around
on the fence, and the cattlemen, they'd auction the
ponies off, eight and nine dollars a head. And then
they'd bring them to the blacksmith shop to have
them shod. Now, they'd paw you. They'd scratch
you or bite you, chew your pants up. You used to
have to tie them up so close to the walls they
couldn't get their heads around, but see, we didn't
have shoeing stocks. We had shoeing ropes. We'd
just rope 'em, throw 'em down, and hog-tie 'em,
and if they broke a leg, all right, if they broke their
necks, all right. But we were lucky—none of them
did break their legs or their necks.

Rick: Did you ever get hurt shoeing?

Rudy: Yeah. I got a horseshoe nail in me one time. Dad
always told me when you shoe a horse, the front
leg you put between your legs and then the back
leg you lay it up here in front of your legs. And he
always told me when the horse was bad and
jerked, as soon as that nail come out, pull the
point up a little, and then I wouldn't get hurt. The
only thing, Dad said, that saved me was the strings
on the apron. The buckskin apron, being rotten,
broke. This horse, I'd shod him before, and he

never had jerked. But I had this nail out, I guess half an inch, and he jerked from the inside and caught me in the groin. Went through the shoeing apron, went in my groin and tore it, and throwed me down. When he got the nail in the apron, he twisted me, but when I went down, the apron string broke and I rolled up. Well, I like to bled to death. But I never had a stitch in it. You know what they done? Dad always kept turpentine in the shop, and they picked me up and took me down in that room where we used to build wagons in the wintertime, and they poured turpentine in there.

And I thought, Well, the leg's gonna come off. I never had anything hurt me as bad in my life— not like that did. Anyway, they picked me up and got me home, laid me on my back. And Dad made his swabs. He went up to the drugstore and bought some cotton. He'd come down there every once in a while and clean that. I was in bed a long time, on my back—but I never did have a stitch put in there. Didn't have a tetanus shot or nothing else. The way it looks now, the scar's about three inches. But back then, he ripped me I bet five inches, plumb across.

Rick: How old were you when it happened?
Rudy: I was about nineteen.
Rick: What would happen if a horse kicked you?
Rudy: Oh well, lots of guys have been killed that way. I've always been lucky. I never was kicked, never would take that chance. I'd see one was gonna kick, I'd throw the rope on that back foot and draw it up there. My dad taught me that from a little boy up.

But going back to the shop. You didn't go to the shop and sit down. You opened the door, you had plenty to do. Back in those days, you never

did catch up. The work just piled up. There was wagon work, buggy work, and horseshoeing. We sharpened plows and cultivator bits. I always stayed in the fire. Once in a while, I'd maybe drive some wagon spokes and put in some fellows, something like that, but I never would fool too much on wagon beds. I made the iron for wagon beds, but I never did no woodwork. And those iron wagon tires. They used to be those old five- or eight-feet wagon tires—those days they had high wheels. Then finally they had them cut down. We used to bend them up and they'd be four in a set. Every tire was marked. And how we remembered that, I don't know, but some way we marked them. Then we'd get a wood fire started, and we'd heat the tires like that. Instead of heating one in the forge, we'd heat maybe four sets at once. We'd had special watering troughs made. Takes lots of water to cool five- or eight-feet wagon tires.

Rick: Big freight wagons?

Rudy: Yeah. And then they had some three-inch tires, three inches wide. But they were only about half an inch thick, all forge welded. We didn't even know what an acetylene or an arc welder was in those days. I've seen my dad weldin' wagon tires. He used sand, real fine white sand. Throw it in there for flux.

I'll tell you another thing, too. This was a railroad town, and these hobos they'd come from St. Louis to Springfield, Missouri, riding freight trains. You could learn a whole lot from them fellas. Dad went and opened the shop one morning in the summer. There's a hobo laying out there beside the shop. Now Dad had a Peter-Wright anvil that had got worn. This hobo said, "If you'll give me some tools, I'll fix it."

Rick: How'd he fix it?

Rudy: Well, he made a big fire. Used the biggest forge and duck's nest [the part of the forge that contains the fire] that was there. And he had a block and tackle and a chain. That ol' anvil weighed about 150 pounds. And when he brought it out of the fire, he had another anvil set there to compare it to. He'd heat one side and he'd take a horseshoe rasp to take off the burrs on that side. Then when he got ready to do the other side, he'd put it back in and let the first side get cold. And he'd keep a-draggin' the anvil in and out of the fire. It seemed like it'd take an hour to get that thing hot. But when he got through, it looked like it came from the factory.

Rick: He didn't forge it down?

Rudy: Oh, no.

Rick: He just hot rasped the high spots off it?

Rudy: Just the high spots. I've heard Dad say that he never saw a man temper like that fella could.

Rick: How'd he temper that anvil face?

Rudy: I don't even know. He didn't want no one to say nothin' to him, not while he was a-workin'. And when he got through, he asked Dad where the bootleggers were around there, so he could get some whiskey. And Dad told him that the town was dry, he didn't know of any bootleggers there at that time. Then he pulled out. He caught a freight train and on he went.

    Back in the thirties, in the depression time, I lived half a block from the shop. Now, our shop had electric lights and the other shops didn't. One night, about nine o'clock, someone knocked and I hollered, "Come in." There stood a man, and he said, "Say, is your name Rudolph Williams?" "Yeah." "And you got 'lectric lights in the shop, haven't you?" "Yeah." "Well," he said, "I'm with Odell Construction Company. We're gonna build a road down here on the river. I wanted to get some blacksmith to do my blacksmithing at night so we could have it ready at seven o'clock to take down to the river." I said, "Well, I could do the work, but I got an awful good bed in here and the weather's pretty bad. I'd have to have pretty good pay, too." He said, "We don't care about the pay, just so we get good work done." I said, "Well, okay, I'll take the job. When do you want me to start?" He said, "Now." He had a load of picks and mattocks and plenty of dipper blades to sharpen. So we went over there and I guess by the time I got started, unloaded, and got the fire built, it was ten o'clock. I went home that morning at four o'clock and I figured I'd made almost forty-nine dollars, made a month's wages in one night. Rick, I thought I was the richest man in my hometown.

Rick: During World War II, you worked down at Fort Leonard Wood, didn't you?

Rudy: Yeah, I was a civil service blacksmith for five years.

Rick: What'd you do down there, primarily?

Rudy: We made hangers, sharpened picks, and sharpened mattocks—but mostly made hangers.

Rick: How long have you had this shop, Rudy?

Rudy: Why, I've had this a little over thirty years.

Rick: What type of work do you do these days?

Rudy: Tool sharpening. These jackhammer points that contractors use to break concrete and rocks. I got thirty-one contractors I work for.

Rick: What type of equipment do you use now, Rudy?

Rudy: I got two good trip-hammers, set on concrete. They weigh about two thousand pounds apiece and have five-horsepower motors on them. They

Photograph of Williams in blacksmith shop, Fort Leonard Wood, 1940s.

help out a whole lot. I hardly ever pick up a hand hammer.

And anvils, they're out of this world now. I used to buy them for five dollars apiece back years ago, but they run high now. You're lucky if you can get one for less than two hundred dollars. They say you can't hardly find anvils. Lots of people go to farm sales specially to find an anvil. I got my anvils chained down. I never done that before in my life. They'd come in and take 'em right off the block. And coal, you can't find no good blacksmith coal no more.

Rick: You don't have an arc welder or acetylene in here, do you?

Rudy: No.

Rick: How fast do you sharpen your points?

Rudy: One jackhammer point a minute, one moil point a minute. Now that's after you get your heat. After I build my fire and get it going good, I put in ten points. The hammer's right there by me and all I gotta do is turn her on, and I sharpen it and temper it at the same heat. I don't have to go back in the fire 'cause you can do it all in one heat.

Rick: You can move fast enough that you can sharpen, harden, and temper them in one heat?

Rudy: Oh yeah. And the main thing about tempering, if you get 'em too soft, ain't no good. And if you get 'em too hard, well of course, they'll break. Now I've been pretty lucky. The contractors would tell you the same thing. I don't have very many of my points break. But lots of them break two inches up. No blacksmith tempers them up that far. And then I got that set of tubs with water in the bottom and holes in the top for these moil points to go in. And when I get my color, they go down in there,

for that temper can't go down or it can't go up.
It's gotta stay right there at the water line.

Rick: Do you like to work by yourself pretty much?

Rudy: I do now. I want to be my own boss. I'm a whole
lot like that hobo was. When I'm a-workin', I
don't like to have too much company. They ask
you questions. Well, you like to answer, you know.
I had a guy here one day. He just asked every kind
of question there was. Finally, I said, "I'm so busy
here and I gotta get this work out. I can't get it
out, stopping to explain things."

If I got work to do, the contractors know ol'
Williams will get it done. If I tell a contractor he
can get his work tomorrow at nine o'clock, he
knows he won't go back after it twice.

Rick: Because you can depend on yourself.

Rudy: Well, I know exactly what to do next. I've been
runnin' a shop about forty-nine years. Back when I
was young, it was a different story. I used to have
two fellows working for me all the time. But old as
I am, I like to come over here and do what I want
to. And if I want to go home, I want to lock up. I
usually go home about one o'clock every day.

This time last year, Rick, a guy, a good contractor, said he was gonna have about two
hundred moil points a day. Had a big job downtown. And after he called me, I first told him I
didn't care whether I got the job or not. Me and
him had a little trouble about pay. Well, he's honest, but sometimes some of them pays when they
wants to. Anyway, we made a deal, twenty-third
day of July up to the fifteenth of September. That
guy brought me all the way from 190 to 215 moil
points every day, and it was hot last year, July and
August. I came over here at six o'clock, and by
nine o'clock I had him a-goin' with the work all

done. Then I'd eat breakfast and go home. I didn't want the job, but after I figured it all out, it was about the best setup I ever had. I got over here while it was early, while it was cool, because that tin roof gets real hot.

When you're young, you know, you can take it. Now when I was eighty years old, my family, my son and my daughter, they said they couldn't see no change in Dad. I could take the heat. I could take the cold. In the summertime, I'd be here maybe nine hours. But you get past eighty, it's a little bit different. But I still thank the Lord that I'm able to go and I feel good. I work every day, Rick, I got a little money, not much, but I'm not working for the money. It's just 'cause I hate to give it up. Now my dad was a blacksmith fifty years, and I've been at it forty-nine years. I thank the Lord every day He lets me stay. I'd like to go fifty years, anyway. And then I don't know. If everything goes good, I might not retire even then.

I've had a good life and I got a good family. I got a good wife and so much to be thankful for. I'm not perfect, but I love the Lord and I realize that He's been good to me. You know as you get older, you sit around and you think about times back. It's just nature, any old man will tell you that. I can remember things that happened back years ago when I was a little kid, but I don't know what I done last year. But that inner mind of the shop will never die in me. It can't die. I couldn't get rid of it. If I could, I wouldn't be here today. That inner mind from a little boy can send my dad's picture. Of course, I loved my dad and he worked hard, and I felt sorry for him. When I was a little boy, he'd come home with a lantern from hammerin' at night, trying to provide a living for Mom, us boys. I regret lots of things I've done in my lifetime, but as far as the shop's concerned, no. It's been my life. There's just something about it, Rick, that's all.

Leslie Ostendorf

Leslie Ostendorf is an agricultural blacksmith in Addieville, Illinois. This interview occurred at his shop, where he has worked for thirty-seven years.

Rick: Did you start here in this shop?

Les: Yeah. I'll tell you what happened. In my younger days, my dad took work as a blacksmith. He used to say, "Why in the hell don't you become a blacksmith? I think you'd make a good one." And I'd say, "Aw, I'd rather farm." Then in later years when I got started over here, he kidded me about that and said, "You got to be one after all, didn't you?" I said, "That sure wasn't my intention." It happened when I got married. When my wife and I got married, we stayed with her father for five years. He had a fairly good farm but he didn't own it, and one day we got a notice we couldn't rent the farm anymore. So there we were—no place to go. You couldn't buy a house or rent one, and that's how we got here to Addieville.

When we came down here, I needed a job. Bill [Les's onetime partner] used to have a bench on the porch. He was here early in the mornings, and he'd sit on the bench and smoke a cigarette. He said, "Come on over and let's have a little talk." He knew my father real well—in fact, he was a distant relative of ours, even had the same last name—and when we moved to Addieville, my dad would come and visit him a lot. He never brought work over, though, 'cause Bill was just a little out of his reach. We had a blacksmith close to home in the same community. One day Bill said to me, "What do you intend to do?" And I said, "Bill, I got no idea yet. I've got to start some place."

Well, I was supposed to start here at the elevator. They had a guy quitting in the spring of the year. We'd moved here in late fall. Then in April, this guy was going to quit and I was supposed to have his job. Bill said if I didn't have anything to do, I could help out here at the blacksmith shop. There wasn't a whole lot I could do, but he said he had a couple of wagon beds to build and even if I didn't know much, he knew I could drive nails! I guess he saw I was fairly handy. One day he said I ought to work steady here. He'd been here by himself all the time and he had a fairly good business, but he wanted somebody to be around. He loved his fishing and hunting, and he just wanted to get away. Well, I said I didn't know if I could get along with it. "Oh heck, yeah," he said, "you'll get along. I'll help you." Well, I took him up on it, and when I went home that morning, I told my wife. She said why didn't I help him out that winter, and if I liked it, I could get going there.

So during the winter months, I stayed and got used to the place. I thought there wasn't much use in going back to the elevator. There's a lot of lifting—you know, sacks—and I haven't got the greatest back anyway. So I went over to the elevator and talked to the guy there, and he said if that's what I had in mind, he was all for me. I made sure there wasn't going to be any hard feelings. Then I told Bill if he wanted me here, I'd stay. "That's fine with me," he said. "I love to go fishin'!" So that's how I got started in the black-smith shop with Bill Ostendorf. Bill had gotten the shop after Brennecke.

Rick: Was Brennecke the original owner?

Les: Yeah, he started the shop in 1892. Brennecke had five sons, but none of those boys ever was a black-smith. They got to be implement dealers—one of 'em started an implement shop, but it didn't last too long. Then they started here when the old fella was gone, but later they got away from it. Then Bill must have started here in the early forties, I'd say. He developed the place. He'd started out with a fellow by the name of Nobey. That's how he learned his trade.

Rick: And you learned the trade from Bill?

Les: Yeah. He was a heck of a nice guy to work with, and we never had words with each other. He might have been mad at me sometimes, but he never raised Cain. I learned a lot from Bill, but a lot of stuff you just have to pick up by yourself. Like he said, "Just mess around with it. Your own practice is as good as any."

We worked like this—one Saturday was his and one was mine. The first year I was here, I was kind of dumb, but he'd say, "Tomorrow's my day off, so if you get anything you can't handle, let it go till I get back. Just do the best you can and tie into it. If it don't work out, it don't work out." That's how I started to learn on the electric welder. I mostly did that when he wasn't around. A lot of times I didn't want to do it, but guys would say, "Oh, you can do it. You got to start sometime." Now today, I claim I'm one of the best welders in Washington County—least that's what people tell me—when it comes to electric welding.

I only had one little problem with Bill. He

really never showed me just how to adjust the acetylene torch. Oh, I saw him sit there a lot, but I'd either have too much air or it'd get too hot. Then your plow would get hot, and it'd sink, and you'd get a hole in it—I had quite a tussle with that. I got along, though. I asked Bill a few times and he said it looked real good, but I never told him how much trouble I had with the heat.

I remember the very first time I used a forge. He put me on some spike harrows. They was thick. I guess we had about fifty of 'em here, maybe more. That's one of the first things I started doing with a forge. Well, he showed me how he worked it under the trip-hammer. It was just like drinking a glass of water for him, but to me, man, it made sweat come. And if you wasn't careful, you'd get 'em too hot and burn 'em. They'd just melt away. Well, that never happened but I was always afraid it would, so I was real careful and I done some sweating for a couple of days. I didn't get that much done. He said, "I don't care how long you mess with it—get used to it!"

Rick: What other kind of work did you and Bill do?

Les: Well, then the next thing come along was the plows. A lot of these farmers were still plowing with horses and gang plows. That's a plow that's got two beams, two moldboards, two shares, and it's got three wheels on it and you hitch four horses to it. A fellow south of town came in one day and brought his plowshares—he had maybe four shares that he'd run dull. I hammered them out—I'd seen a little of how Bill had done it.

Well, this fellow came and picked up his plowshares. He took 'em home and in a few days he came back and said, "Bill, these plowshares don't stay in the ground right. They come right

out." Well, I felt a little bad 'cause I thought I'd done a good job. And when he was gone, I said, "Bill, look 'em over so I know exactly what I did wrong." "Well," he said, "I don't have to look 'em over. I know they're all right. You're a new fellow, and the old guy just had that in his head. All you do is take all four shares, pitch 'em in the fire, and burn 'em black. He'll come and pick 'em up, and you'll never see him back again." And that's just what happened. Later on I saw him, and he said, "Oh, they run good!"

Bill was a heck of a good guy, but don't you ever get him riled. A guy came over one day who had his own welder. He said, "Bill, the dang stuff don't hold. You gotta put a bolt in it to make it work." Bill says, "You want it bolted or you want it welded?" He says, "I want both." Bill says, "Then I won't do it. I'll weld it or I'll bolt it, but I won't do both. When I weld it, it'll be welded. None of this smearing around on it." Well, the guy didn't like it, but he said, "Okay, weld it." Bill said, "Now if it breaks, you bring it back and there won't be any charge to fix it." Well, the guy never brought it back, but Bill sure did get mad when he wanted it welded and bolted in the same spot.

Rick: So you did a lot of repair work?

Les: Yeah, a lot. Now horseshoeing, that's something I never got into. Bill did in his earlier days, not while I was here. At the time I came, you needed a license for that or you'd have to have a veterinarian standing by you watching. Then you could get by with it. We had a fellow here with a license, and he had it in for us. He didn't have much work, you see. Bill said if I'd start shoeing a horse and he'd find out about it, he'd put it to us. And he would have! But Brennecke's, some of these old-timers told me, they had men who'd put shoes on. Farmers would come to town and drop their milk at the milk station, then go on and do their shopping. You didn't have automobiles like today and the roads weren't that good, so they'd try to do all their business in one trip to town.

Rick: Well, when you've had experience with farming and opportunities for other jobs, I wonder why you'd want to stick with blacksmithing. It's not the easiest job in the world.

Les: No, that it isn't! I would have liked to have had my own farm, but there was no way I could get it. I was the oldest in the family, and I got married and that was it.

When we got here, I needed a job. I always did like to do something—I didn't like to sit around. And I guess I just took a liking to working here. Like my dad says, heck, you don't have to drive, you can walk across the street, go home for lunch, you don't wear out your automobile. What my intention was, I really wanted to paint. I did love to paint. My dad has a cousin who was a terrific painter. He worked for my father when he had his farm, and I learned quite a bit from him. He taught me a lot of tricks of painting and staining and graining. But he said one day in German, "Aw, that's just plain dumb, you wanting to be a painter. You better stay with this."

Then I thought, too, I grew up on the farm, and a lot of guys coming down here, they were raised in the city or a small community and they didn't know what a pitchfork was or a shovel or anything like that. But I knew what all that was, and I knew about the horse-drawn farm machinery. We had a lot of them coming in those years, and I knew what they were and what you could do with them and what you couldn't. That helped me a lot.

Farm life to me was just as easy, and you didn't have to aggravate yourself with the public. But I must say I got a pretty good bunch of people I'm working for. Oh, there's some you'd just as soon not see 'em come, but most of my customers are real nice people. They're not going to bug you to death. If it's a must and they need it bad, I can see doing it for 'em and they know that. Even that time when I was hurt and didn't work for eight months, I had the customers come up to the house and visit me.

Rick: What happened?

Les: Well, I was changing these rotary mower blades— a lot of fellows call 'em brush hogs, I call 'em a rotary chopper—and I had the mower lifted up and a pair of steel sawhorses set underneath the back end. We always put them under there for protection. That brand of mower has got such a dad-gummed poor setup when it comes to changing the rotary blades. When they come out with it, they give you a little wrench like a toy wrench. Then when you use your mower one season—it's got those hex nuts on it—and with the weeds and stuff you can't hold the nut with that wrench. You've got those fine threads, and it's a left-hand thread, and you can't get 'em off. It's confusing— which way you're gonna go, which way you're not gonna go. And this guy, he argued with me. He said, "Oh, these ain't left-hand." I said, "Sure it is. I've taken too many off." He said, "Oh, it can't be." But it was and they wouldn't come off. I heated them and I cooled them. Then I crawled underneath, and the hydraulic lines broke and the mower fell on me. It pushed the sawhorses' legs down in the soft dirt and pinned me underneath, and he said, "Don't move. I'll get an ambulance. You're hurt bad."

He was right. I had hurt my back real bad. I laid there five days in the hospital with no sleep. And I had so many visitors come that I told the nurse and my wife I don't want to see none of my friends. They meant good and wanted to see me, but I hurt too bad to have company. I laid there five days, and then I told the doctor, "Gee whiz, I've got a cracked rib." "No," he said, "it can't be. The X rays didn't show it." My old doctor came around a day or two later and I told him, "I've got a broken rib. I know I have because I've had 'em before and I know how they hurt." Well, he didn't say much. He just kind of stared at you. Then he said, "Okay, we'll take care of it." So they took another X ray and that showed it. Well, I could have stayed another week or two, but my doctor said, "All you've got to do is just lay." Which I did. So in other words, for the way I've been hurt, it don't bother me too much. It hurts me the worse when we go on a trip, sittin' in the car. That hurts my back more than my work here, unless I do a lot of heavy lifting.

Rick: You keep a very neat shop, which I've often admired. Do you find it easier to work that way?

 Les: Oh yeah, I don't like things messed up. Even like now when we're remodeling a little bit, we're messed up more than I like it, with this lumber laying here, but that's the only way we can do it. Yesterday I had that whole bench laying full of tools from one end to the other, but before I went home last night for supper, they was all cleaned up.

Rick: Nowadays, what kind of work do you do?

Hammering out mower blades

Les: Every day I run into a different type of work. It's never the same—some days I really enjoy it and others I wish I'd stayed home!

Well, years back we had a lot of plowshares to be sharpened, but today it has let up a little, though there's still quite a few. The chisel plows have kind of taken over, and then these throwaway blades, throwaway plowshares. Generally, they put 'em on, and they run 'em so thick and all. Then they pitch 'em—throw 'em away. Some people bring 'em in and have 'em hammered out thin and have a hard surface put on 'em. But getting back to the old style plowshare, I do like to work on them. We put 'em in a forge, get 'em hot and hammer a point on 'em, run 'em over a grinder and hard surface 'em. If they don't want the hard surface, we generally temper 'em good and hard so they'll last.

I still do a lot of plow work and harrow sharpening, still get some throwaway plowshares, cultivator sweeps, and a lot of repair on farm implements, maybe changing gears or welding the weak spots or reinforcing with an extra piece of iron. You know a lot of stuff at the factories is just slapped together. Or else they put such a poor weld job on it that it doesn't stay put. It's not really blacksmithing anymore because of all the mechanical work—working on gears or putting in new chains or repairing holes in truck beds.

Rick: What time do you start work?

Les: Oh, lots of times I come over about six o'clock. I mess around for a little bit, then go across the street for coffee and breakfast. Then I come back. I work like a young one. My boy, he's thirty-seven years old and I work with him. He sometimes works later at night than I do, but I'm over here practically every night till nine o'clock. We have supper around six o'clock, and in the busy season I come back.

When Bill and I was here together and it got to be twelve o'clock, he would leave all the doors wide open and go home for an hour. Then when it got to be five o'clock, he'd say, "Well, it's five o'clock. We'll do the rest tomorrow, if there's another day. If there's no other day, we just won't have to do it!"

Nowadays, though, if I get a guy and he's broke down, I'll stay with it till it's done unless things get in too much of a mess. Today, it's real peaceful here, but yesterday and the day before, it was terrible. I didn't get no time to relax at all. I kind of enjoy it, though. I'd as soon come down of an evening and mess around here instead of watch television. I get just as much enjoyment coming here. It's just rooted into me.

Hard surfacing a plowshare

Darold Rinedollar

*Darold Rinedollar, a blacksmith for
approximately twenty-five years, has established a
diversified business including both horseshoeing and
commission work. He was interviewed in his shop
in Augusta, Missouri.*

Rick: When did you get started in this, Darold?

Darold: Well, I was always interested in blacksmithing or
some sort of ironwork even when I was a little kid.
My dad used to take me down to what they called
the "drop-forge" in Rockford, Illinois. It was a big
building, and these huge machines would come and
mash an ingot about a foot in diameter, and the
whole building and the ground would shake.

Rick: Impressive?

Darold: Sure was. Then as I was growing up, I worked
with horses and I started to shoe them. I went to
vet's school to learn a little more about it because I
was going to shoe race horses and show horses.
They're very expensive animals, and I wanted to
make sure I could handle any problem I'd run into.

Rick: Did your family have horses?

Darold: Yes, we always had some horses. At one time, we
had a riding stable, a show stable, and we had
about twenty-eight head.

Rick: Was that around here, around the St. Louis area?

Darold: That was in Princeton, Illinois. One of the horseshoers that used to come out when I was growing
up was a real character. He'd let me fool with his

forge, and he brought out a forge one time for my birthday.

Rick: What birthday was this?

Darold: Oh, I guess I was ten or twelve years old because I remember that was the best birthday. I spent the whole day out there getting dirty and hammering around, sweating. Then later I went to Ithaca, New York, to Cornell University Vet School. There were a couple of old-timers there who were blacksmiths. They had an old shop in one of those little towns in the hills, and I used to go see them just because they were such characters, and I got to talking to them. Gradually, they let me do more and more around the shop. They were from Germany, and they showed me a lot of things that were done the old way. They said there wasn't much steel, but they had plenty of time. Of course, I started talking about horseshoes. They'd take a horseshoe and straighten it out, fold it almost in two, insert a new piece of steel in the middle of it and fire weld it together, then draw it back out into a horseshoe and punch holes in it. I think they got fifty or seventy-five cents to shoe a horse. The way they did things, they had old bellows, and they showed me different things with the bellows. That stuck with me. Before that, I'd had people show me things, but they took me under their wings. They said, "Come on in here," and they took time with me. I think that I wasn't under their feet all the time. I was there for a little while, and then they got rid of me. And then I'd come back again. They did restoration work for Old Sturbridge Village.

Rick: What were their names?

Darold: One was Gene and the other was Fred. I never did quite get the relationship. Both of their last names were Forbes. They weren't brothers, but they came from the same area in Germany. They talked with such a dialect that I didn't understand all the things they said, and then of course the German would slip out once in a while. They had some oxen that they used for parades, and I got to shoe those. A lot of the old pieces they were restoring I got to help them either strike or work on. I learned the old methods actually by helping them and going along with them, which is better than just watching somebody. They were such characters—they made little jokes about doing it this way and that way.

Rick: That would help you remember it, too. They sound like good teachers really. How long did you work with them?

Darold: Just a short time while I was going to school. It was only about a year that I was out there. That was back when the Cuban Missile Crisis happened, and I got drafted. Of course, that interrupted school. It wasn't a regular veterinary school where you covered everything. I just wanted to study the horse part of it, and they gave me special teachers. I was getting blacksmithing and horseshoeing both, kind of a cram course.

Rick: Do you think you were self-taught, too, through books and experimentation?

Darold: Yeah, mostly. And what I remembered from the old-timers. Whenever I see any old blacksmiths, I ask them if I can work with them or observe them, and I go to workshops. But mostly it's trial and error, I guess. You can see something and somebody can tell you something. But to do it the way that it pleases you, that's totally different. You're constantly trying to improve or change things.

Rick: What type of work do you do now, Darold? I see gates and ornamental work here in the shop.

Antique wagons ready for restoration work

Darold: Well, we do gates and fencing. We do fireplace tools, kitchen pot racks. We do some of the old restoration work like trivets and things from museums, restoration projects. We do some work on carriages, restoration on those. We shoe a few horses and do repair sometimes. I guess you'd say just a little bit of everything. Every day there's something different, new challenges.

Rick: You do a little production work, a few bread and butter items like everybody else does, and then the commission work?

Darold: We have a mail-order business. We produce the corn dryers like they were done originally. Then we sell hooks and things that we advertise in a couple of national magazines.

Rick: I'd say from looking at your work, that you follow a fairly traditional approach. The whole shop is pleasing. It's like a museum as well as a shop.

Darold: Well, I like working with the old tools. Most of my customers have a lot of money, and they want something a little different than the next fellow down the road. They want to be able to say, "I had this made." You can't do a lot of these things with modern tools. You've got to do it the old traditional way. That's how I build my business, doing it that way.

When you're working on a restoration project, you have to think how the blacksmith would have been thinking back in the 1800s or the 1700s, with the tools that they had. If you use those tools, you would have to think that way because there are no modern tools to short-cut with. Your approach starts out different, and the piece ends up different. From the old-timers I've worked with and as much restoration work that I've done, I really like that approach. I like just the simple lines, not so ornate.

Most of the designs we make are our own ideas. We might have seen an old one that we got an idea from, but we went on from there with it.

Rick: I think every blacksmith I've ever known went through a replication of historical work to learn the techniques. Making tomahawks, chain links, all the things that were made in the past even though there may not be too much of a need for those anymore. It's an exercise so that you can understand the old procedures.

Darold: It's a discipline. You learn that you have to do it this way, whether you want to or not, to get that effect.

Rick: In the blacksmith shop the material, the fire, and the tools dictate your procedure. You have to follow the material. You have to think ahead.

Darold: When you see some of the things that were made back in the twelfth and thirteenth centuries and the tools they had to do it with, you know, it's amazing what they came up with. It's a real challenge even nowadays to come close with the modern tools.

Rick: Of course, they probably had unlimited time.

Darold: Yes. I've done some research on that, just on account of the type of things I make. I try to figure what history was involved in it. A lot of the pieces were done by blacksmiths that were hired by well-to-do families. They took care of the blacksmith. They'd say, "Okay, we want this done, and there's no set time on it. We'll take care of you for the rest of your life if need be. You just go ahead with that job."

Rick: Yes, for instance, some cathedrals took six hundred years to build. Perhaps six generations of blacksmiths worked on one cathedral all of their lives. They did the big grillwork, the gates, the

Stoking his bellows forge

hinges, the work on the inside, whatever, kept the masons' tools sharp. Time was viewed differently back then.

Darold: Now it's totally the reverse. Now, you have to think about how fast you can do something in order to come out even. You don't get the same effect. You can't take the pride in the work. Yet, the more hammering you put on a piece, the more you refine the steel you're working on. It strengthens it as well as gives it a nice appearance. The twists and things all make it stouter. Once you start on a project, it just sort of builds. You can work forever on one piece if you want to.

Still, we use some of the modern tools. We couldn't do it all by hand or people couldn't afford it. A lot of things I do I don't charge the people for, because I want to do it that way as a challenge or whatever. I just like the effect. But you have to cut some corners. Instead of fire welding everything, maybe you weld some things, like a big fence project, with the arc welder.

Rick: You and I both know that it takes a lot of helpers to do things in the traditional way. In the old days, they had a lot of people around. They could say, "Okay fellows, we're going to put this big gate into the fire, and we're going to take a heat in this one spot," instead of using a cutting torch with a rosebud tip on it where one man can do it instead of three or four men lifting a huge, heavy gate. There are other reasons for using modern tools like the cost of labor now.

Remember the big controversy? It doesn't seem to be raging anymore, but there was the purest controversy against the modern technological tools. The question was, "Are you really a blacksmith if you're using arc welders and other modern ma-

Demonstration at a craft fair

chines?" I think that's been pretty well settled. Almost everybody has modern machinery in their shops now.

Darold: I think it depends on what you want to make. If you want to make strictly traditional stuff, then you use the traditional tools. If you want to compromise a bit, you use a little of both. It just depends what you want to work on. I like some of the contemporary things that are done well. Some of them are very pleasing, very intricate. I like seeing them, and there's a place for them. But I'm kind of stuck in my role.

Rick: It's your expression.

Darold: Yes. Don't get me wrong. I'm not saying this is the only way to do it. It all has a place, and there's some beautiful contemporary work out. I personally can't do it, though. I don't have that type of design feeling inside me. But we can't be stuck in one particular place and time. You have to bounce around a little to keep your mind alert. You can't just stagnate and say, "This is all I'm going to look at and all I'm going to do." I've done some art nouveau and some contemporary pieces. Every time you do a piece, you know you can do the next one better. This keeps building all the time.

Rick: Do you enjoy the physical aspect of the work?

Darold: Yes, I really do. I've always liked sports and physical exercise, and this is one way to get plenty of it. It's a good, honest feeling. You're dirty, you're sweaty, but you got it honestly.

Rick: Why did you become a blacksmith?

Darold: I just get satisfaction out of doing it. I get paid more by the inner feelings than I ever do by the money. The money is secondary on a job, really. You need the money to survive, but just seeing the job done is first. It's a challenge. You keep building

more and more challenges into each piece. When you get done, you think, "Well, I got that accomplished. I'm going to challenge myself a little more next time." It's a game you play with yourself—to see what it would take to stump you, I guess.

I really get satisfaction out of taking a bar of steel and making it into something useful. When you get done with it, no matter what you get for the piece, even if you give it away, you can't put a price on what you feel inside. When I do a nice piece of work, or what I think is nice, there's a satisfaction I get that I can't get doing any other job—and I've done quite a few of them. This seems to be a little bit of everything. You have to design the piece, you have to make it, you have to engineer it so it's going to work right, and when it's all done, it has to be pleasing. It has to please you as well as other people. I just won't do anything that doesn't please me. If somebody comes in and wants me to make something and I don't like the looks of it, I won't do it, because when it gets done I won't have a good feeling about it. Maybe that's crazy, but that's just the way I am. I get just as much satisfaction out of seeing the finished piece as anything else. And then seeing the people that really like it, to watch their faces when they see it.

Rick: It's a communication between you and them.

Darold: Yes. They usually let me do the design. They give me some suggestions of what they like, maybe look through some drawings or something and give me a couple of basic ideas. Then I'll sketch it up, or I'll just do the piece and see how they like it. You put part of yourself into whatever you do. You drive by and you see some gates that you've done and you say, "Those are my gates. Even though they belong to somebody else, they're still my

gates. There's a lot of me in there. I remember what it took to do this or that on them."

My wife will call me on the phone and say, "Do you know what time it is?," and I'll say, "No, I don't,"—and I really don't. She'll say, "It's three o'clock in the morning." She didn't know whether something had happened to me. Well, you just get lost. When you're doing something, you get another idea. There's just not enough time in your lifetime to do everything that you have ideas for. Your work is endless, and you never can learn it all. You can't even scratch the surface. One thing opens up another door to somewhere else. You can't work fast enough to accomplish it. I know some people who go to factory jobs and stuff. All they look forward to is getting out of work. I really miss it if I don't come in here. If I go somewhere, I feel antsy. I just want to get back and go to work.

Daryl Meier

Daryl Meier has been a blacksmith for approximately twenty-one years and is best known for his rediscovery of Damascus or pattern-welded steel. A general blacksmith, he specializes in making knives. He lives near Carbondale, Illinois, and was interviewed in the blacksmith shop at Southern Illinois University, Carbondale.

Rick: Daryl, could you tell me when you started black-smithing?

Daryl: Well, I don't have any specific date that I can point to. When I was a little kid, I was interested in it and I played in the backyard. I had my mother's vacuum cleaner hooked up and a hole dug in the ground. Then I ran the vacuum cleaner hose, and I had a little charcoal fire, and I played around with a section of railroad rail or some such thing. And I did some "blacksmithing"; that is, I hammered some hot pieces. Never amounted to anything, and I lost interest as I went on through formal education.

Since I was twelve years old, I've been involved with muzzle-loading rifles, very interested in shooting, not as a target thing, but the idea of shooting them and hunting with them. In the mid-sixties, I was in a club with other people who felt the same way. It's a little different now, but at that time, if you wanted to have a good-looking gun and a powder horn, shooting bag, and all the things that you would have had if you existed a couple hundred years ago, you just about had to make most of them because there was no source for you to buy them. So everybody started making powder horns, hunting knives, and so forth. I got involved in several of those crafts, and I finally decided it would be better for me to specialize in blacksmithing and barter my blacksmith work for leather work or horn work or whatever else I might need. I started making tomahawks, throwing knives, and patch knives. Once I got started, then I did graduate, in terms of accumulation of equipment, so I could do different kinds of things: better equipment, bigger anvil, better hammers, and so on.

Rick: You had a shop in Carbondale?

Daryl: At that time, yes.

Rick: In the back of your house?

Daryl: Right. My first forge was made in a thirty-gallon barrel that was designed to use charcoal, and that was in the garage of our house. Then we moved. There was no garage there, so I built a building just for the shop.

Rick: Could you tell me who taught you your trade?

Daryl: Well, I didn't have any particular person that I studied under for any length of time. I did a lot of reading—old books and how-to books. Also, when I got started, the only contemporary book that had any how-to information was the Alex Bealer book.

Rick: *The Art of Blacksmithing*?

Daryl: Right. That book has been influential, although I was involved in blacksmithing before I ever ran across it. It's an inspirational book, a romantic book, and it just reads well. It's uplifting to read, and it gives you a sense of—I don't know how to say it—confidence almost. He makes things seem

simple enough that you feel like you could accomplish them. So I'd say that Alex Bealer was an influence.

Rick: You basically did the landmark Damascus research—you, Bob Griffith, and Jim Wallace. [Damascus or pattern-welded steel is made of dissimilar alloys of iron, forge-welded together and manipulated through punch marks, twisting, engraving, and/or acid etching so that a pattern of the various alloys is visible.]

Daryl: Yeah. It's a real interesting situation. When I got started with Damascus, I didn't know anybody else in the whole country that was doing it. I couldn't find anybody. It turns out that there were one or two other people who were teaching themselves, and apparently, the knowledge of how to do this stuff had been carried all along, because since then I've found people whose fathers had taught them. But I never could identify them, and I don't know for sure when I started making the stuff, whether I started it before I met Ivan Bailey [a nationally known artist blacksmith] or not. But Ivan Bailey gave a demonstration at Lumpkin, Georgia, the first time that we met down there in May of 1972. Anyway I got started.

Rick: And you developed it highly.

Daryl: Well, I got real interested in it and read everything I could find, which was very little. I was strongly influenced by Cyril Stanley Smith [author of *A History of Metallography*] and also by Jerzy Piaskowski from Poland. He's a metallurgist in Cracow, Poland. I ran across an article he had written, and I corresponded with him. His hobby is ancient technology. He's done a lot of research on ancient artifacts and their metallurgical examination. He dissects them, does other metallographic

Right, letter opener with Damascus pattern; *far right,* detail of letter opener showing Damascus pattern

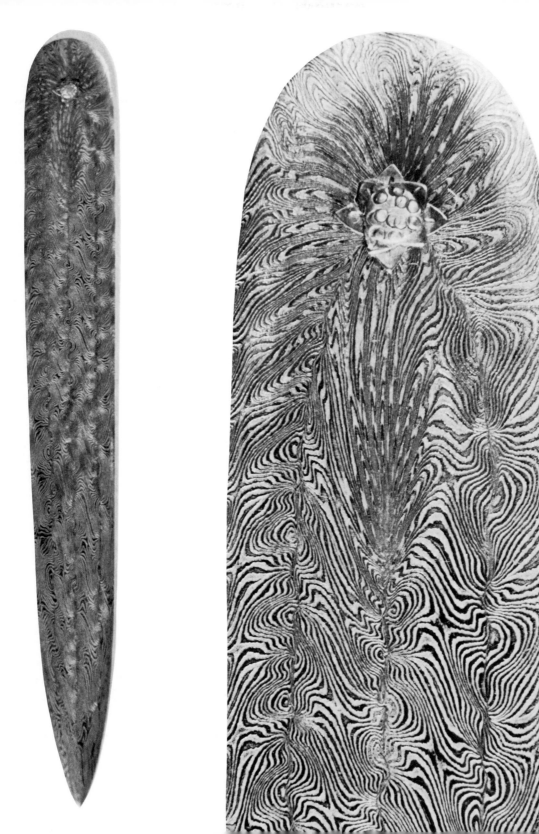

examinations of them, finds out what their composition is, and then makes suppositions about how they were put together. I corresponded with him, and he's a very nice gentleman. I'd write a letter with three questions and receive a letter with three answers, but the answers and the questions didn't quite match 100 percent.

I just worked by trial and error and I asked people questions, not about pattern welding so much as about the techniques that are involved, like forge welding, fluxing, and fire building, and I built up information. And then sometime subsequent to that, I was in the SIU program here at the Graduate School. I was making pattern-welded steel, and then Jim Wallace and Bob Griffith came as graduate students, and at that time, neither one of them had been interested in it; that is, they hadn't done anything on their own. So I remember they saw me making it, and they stopped and looked at what I was doing and said, "Hey, you're going to have to show us how to do that." I remember that I showed them everything I knew in one afternoon in about two hours, although it had taken me nearly two years to learn.

So, in other words, I was at a very elementary level. Then the three of us became just like little kids. Every time one of us would find something out, we couldn't wait to go show the other two. Between the three of us, we learned quite a bit in a very short period of time. We picked up a lot of knowledge, and then after that, we were approached by Dona Meilach to write something about it for her book [*Decorative and Sculptural Ironwork*], which we did as a committee. We each wrote sections of it, and then the other two would review the sections that were done and argue

Damascus billets at forge (lower right)

around until we were all pretty well satisfied. So that was a significant thing. That was the only work on "how to make pattern-welded steel" that had ever been published in modern times. Since then we've all gone our own ways, but I stayed in it; that is to say, it's still the major portion of my activities.

Rick: What type of work do you do now?

Daryl: I teach blacksmithing at SIU. I'm an adjunct instructor. It's a temporary situation, and I'm also part-time, a 25 percent assignment.

Anyway, I've still been doing a lot of research in pattern welding. I found out early on that the pattern-welded steel I was making didn't have magic properties; that is to say, when you're done making it, if you quench it and don't temper it, it's not pliable. It couldn't bend and spring back, so I figured maybe I didn't know as much about it as I'm supposed to. I got to looking into that, and the reason for it is in the carbon. Once you start out with two different kinds of steel that have a different carbon content, in forge welding or in any subsequent hot work, like more welding for other seams or forging, the conditions are right for the carbon to diffuse from the high concentration to the low, and it'll try to equalize itself.

Rick: Just like all other matter?

Daryl: Right. Then I found that on certain historic pieces that wasn't the case. They show a very distinct distribution or integrity of carbon. One layer will have it and one layer won't, and so I've been trying to find out the solution to that problem, that is, how I can make mine so it doesn't diffuse. I've been working on that for eight years or more.

Right, dagger with Damascus pattern; *far right,* detail of dagger showing Damascus pattern

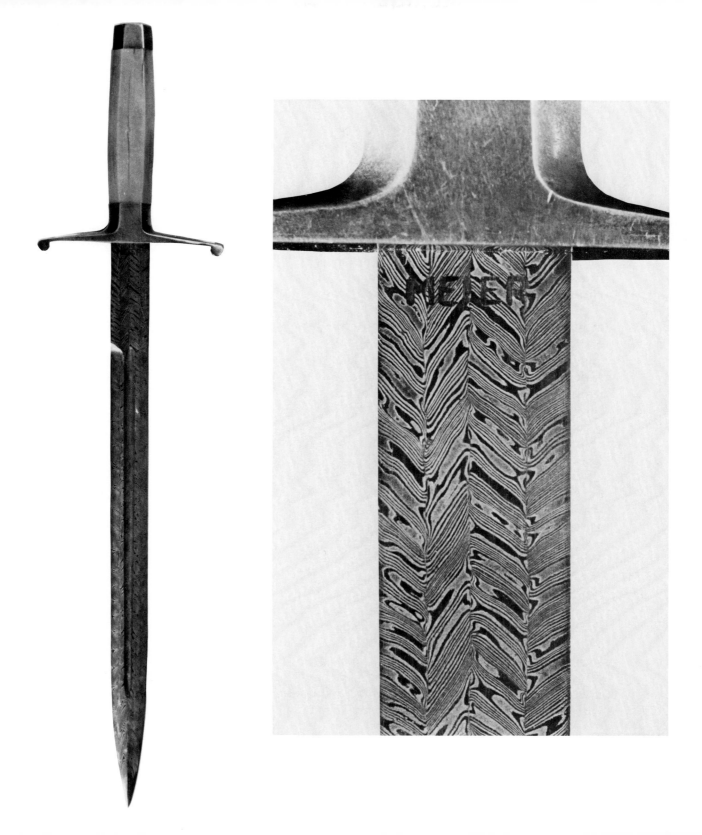

Rick: How are you researching? You learned to read some German and French or some other languages, didn't you?

Daryl: I don't really read anything except German, and I don't read that very well. I've been able to understand a little bit of the vocabulary in German, and I've read some publications in German or attempted to read them, and I've talked to metallurgists who also have an interest in ancient technology. One was a professor emeritus at MIT who was at the University of Chicago for a number of years.

Rick: It sounds like you're very interested in the history of technology. What part of the past are you studying now?

Daryl: The Merovingian period. It's the earliest example of pattern-welded steel that's highly refined that I know of, but I don't think Merovingian people invented it. There's evidence of it being done earlier. The Merovingian period runs roughly from about A.D. 400 to A.D. 650.

Rick: Were the Merovingians in Europe?

Daryl: Yes. South central Europe. Merovingian is a Germanic culture but it got as far west as France and also into what is now eastern Europe. The more information I uncover about these ancient people, the more respect I have for them as craftsmen. I've had the same experience that most of us have. We go through the contemporary American education system, which gives us the idea that anybody that lived before 1925 was basically uncivilized, but I find some of the work done in the fifth and sixth centuries amazing. People didn't have a written language in Merovingian culture or if they did, it was known to so few it didn't count. Maybe a few of them could converse in a nonnative written language like Latin or whatever. There's some evidence of Latin characters appearing on some of their work, but anyway, they made some fabulous stuff and they were doing things without modern technology. I find it difficult for me to do today what they did, and in some cases, I haven't been able to.

Rick: Could you tell me about your work as a blacksmith?

Daryl: I find in my own work that when I accept jobs that are outside my special area of interest, I don't have the proper tooling or the experience to bring them off well. I know the general necessities. I know how to do the job in theory, just basic process. In other words, the guy says, "Can you make something for me?," and I say, "Sure," but I don't have the experience of working in that scale to understand all the problems, which when I get into them, become big and I don't have the specific tools.

The latest thing that happened to me is that a guy wanted me to make him a dozen **S**-shaped pieces that fit on the end of a brick or stone building. They're the ends of tie rods that run longways through the building, the simplest thing in the world. Take a piece of stock, punch a hole in the middle, swell it out where the hole is, draw it down, and bend it into an **S**. What could be more simple? But before I could actually start on that two-hour job, I had eight hours tied up in tooling. That's because I'm not set up for that kind of work. Altogether the job should have taken, on each piece, less than half an hour, but I essentially had three days tied up in it. If an order came along now for another dozen of them, I could make them in a reasonable length of time, but I'm not geared

up for that kind of work load and I didn't antici-
pate that big a problem when I accepted it because
I don't have that much experience working heavier
stock.

Rick: Why did you become a blacksmith?

Daryl: I don't really know. At the time when I got involved initially, it was a hobby. I did it some evenings but mostly weekends, and I worked in
various types of business administration jobs as a
vocation. Sometime after I got involved in blacksmithing, I found that I was getting more satisfaction on a personal basis out of my handwork than
I was out of my brain work and my administration
responsibilities. I took another look at the concept
that we're supposed to amount to something or be
somebody here, make some contribution to society,
or amass a bunch of wealth, or whatever the hell it
is. So I chose to make a living out of blacksmithing. Over a period of years, I've gotten to the point
when I was almost making a living blacksmithing.
I'm not now, so the last couple of years have been
very bad on me. My main business was the tomahawks. That's purely a luxury item although it's
classified technically as a tool. The population
doesn't buy them when they don't have money,
and right now they don't have money.

As to your question about why, I guess that
over a period of time it's just been that I'm trying
to limit my activities to only doing what I enjoy
and hoping that activity will generate an income. I
haven't compromised very much. The only really
highly successful people who make a lot of money
are the ones who've achieved a very famous stature, and the number of those in relation to all the
people practicing in the field appears to be less
than one-tenth of 1 percent.

Rick: But you've already achieved at least a national reputation and probably international.

Daryl: That's true, but the problem is that there are a lot of people who know about my work, but very few of them actually buy any of it. Most of the reputation that I have in my particular field is among other people who have a special interest, and they're involved in doing it themselves rather than in being consumers. Also, they don't have the kind of money it takes to buy my work. So it's a strange thing. Almost everyone throughout the United States who is involved in pattern-welded steel for any length of time either knows me or has heard of me. But they're not the buyers or the collectors. Also, I'm not a salesman, I'm a blacksmith. I think like a blacksmith, and when I lay the hammer down, I lose interest. When I see I've accomplished what I wanted to as far as hammering is concerned, I'm done.

Rick: How about pattern development in Damascus steel?

Daryl: The consumer isn't knowledgeable enough in general to appreciate the work I do; that is, there are a number of people making pattern-welded steel wanting to compare their stuff with mine. Theirs isn't as sophisticated, but the general person who's bought some of their stuff doesn't know enough about the techniques of how it's made to determine whether it's an accomplishment or not, only the basic idea that it's pattern welding. Most, not all, of the successful pattern-welding people don't make any sophisticated patterns, and their success comes from their ability to market their products. To be a successful pattern welder, you have to make what the consumer wants. I more or less make what I want to make, and what I want to make and what the consumer wants don't necessarily turn out to be the same thing.

Another reason why I and a lot of other people went into blacksmithing years ago is that we were concerned that all the skills that were accumulated over several thousand years were going to pass out of the picture, but we've gone past that. It won't happen. There's always something lost with every generation, but with the Artist-Blacksmiths' Association of North America and other organizations it has helped to inspire, there are thousands of people now who are storehouses for knowledge. So I think that we've already accomplished what was needed. I think that we're seeing a resurrection of interest in crafting. I don't think we started it, blacksmiths per se, but we're involved in it and I think we've offered to carry it through. Two or three generations from now, I think that handcraft and blacksmith items are going to be much more prevalent. I think you're going to see much more architectural kind of work.

Rick: You know, this last year there have been several job openings in blacksmith shops around the county. Five or ten years ago that was unheard of.

Daryl: One thing that I've always felt in relation to blacksmithing is that you can't store it in a book. It has to be stored in the living mind and arms. Other parts, too. You can't write a description of a color, and color is very important to blacksmithing. You can read all the old books and they tell you "cherry red" for a certain operation. So what does that mean? When I was a kid growing up, there was a cherry tree in the backyard, and we picked cherries to make pies. When they were ripe, usually one side was yellow and one side was red. Since then I've been buying cherries, and I like these

sweet cherries they call Bings and they're black.
The only way you can convey a color is with a
color chart, which isn't as good as the real thing.
When you've got a person standing there at the
fire, and you say, "See that right there," then that's
it.

Anyway, I'm not researching this stuff because
I see a pot of gold at the end. I just want to find
out, and I can't answer that question of why I'm
interested. I just am. It's like, well, I like trees,
I like to look at trees. I like to be around trees.
I can't explain why. I grew up around trees and
I just like them. I just got hooked on this, and
I'm going to stay with it until I pass out of
the picture.

Meier's shop

L. Brent Kington

L. Brent Kington, *a blacksmith for seventeen years, is a professor of art and the director of the School of Art at Southern Illinois University, Carbondale. He was interviewed at his home studio in Makanda, Illinois.*

Rick: Brent, can you tell me about your early experience in blacksmithing, how you got started?

Brent: I'd be happy to. I've always been very interested in metal. I studied jewelry and metalsmithing as an undergraduate as well as a graduate student. I graduated with my master's degree in 1961. In '64 I spent a significant amount of time in New York City for the first time and studied the Arms and Armor Collection at the Metropolitan Museum of Art. Not that I was really interested in defensive or offensive weapons, but for the first time I was able to see how ferrous metals are used. Now we're all used to seeing ferrous metals used in building construction, automobiles, machines, and so forth, but I saw the material being used in a broad cross section of ways that really interested me, especially the forming and the joining processes and the surface embellishment. And it was an essential viewing experience for me as an artist. As a matter of fact, it was so important that when I got back to Carbondale, I told my wife I was going to be a blacksmith, and I did start acquiring information toward that end. I didn't get around to making a full commitment to the medium until 1970. So it was a six-year gap from the time I became highly influenced by the collection at the Metropolitan until I made a full commitment. There were a number of reasons for that. The work I was doing in the sixties was very much in demand, and I was showing a great deal. Commercial sales—through galleries and exhibitions—were excellent, and I hadn't exhausted the idea that I was interested in. However, as I continued with that work, I sought out blacksmiths in this area, and I started acquiring reading material. There was really very little that had been published on the art of blacksmithing that we didn't have in our library. During that six-year period, I interviewed blacksmiths from Kansas to North Carolina. I felt the best way to assemble information was to talk to people and see how things were done.

Rick: Were you based in Carbondale then?

Brent: Yes. I came to Carbondale in 1961 as a junior faculty member. So anyway I acquired information and started assembling tools that I knew I would need. I started off with very little background or information. I was a trained silversmith, so I essentially knew how to use hammers and certain tools that did relate to the smithing process. But I had to find a complete shop—forge, anvil, hammer, tongs, fullers, swedges—which was fun because most of those tools had been junked and nobody wanted them. I can remember one purchase that I made in St. Louis of a 185-pound anvil, twelve pairs of tongs, a blacksmith's cone, swedging block, three large raising stakes, and a blower—all for thirty-four dollars. I paid something in the neighborhood of a half cent a pound for the whole deal. They didn't want to melt the stuff down and nobody

Right, *Cruciform;* **far right,** *Cruciform*

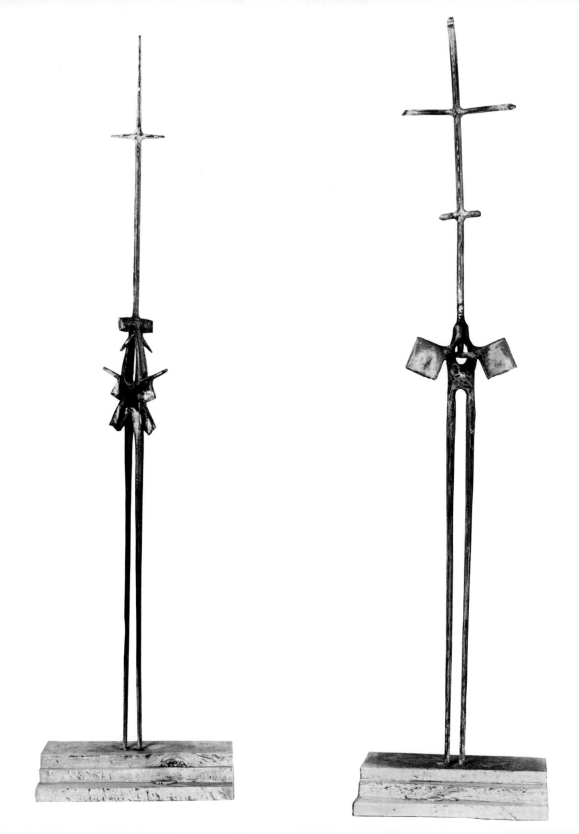

else wanted it, so I was able to secure a good buy. Anyway, my interests grew as I acquired tools and information. I was taking welding classes and beating a lot of metal up at the anvil. Until then most of my work had been very small, dealing with precious metals, silver and gold. I had very clear definitions of my imagery and my personal aesthetics in my other work, and I think probably my two greatest challenges were getting used to a different scale and trying to figure out what I wanted to do with the medium.

In blacksmithing I had to develop a different sense of scale, a different work methodology. I didn't know how to gas weld or arc weld. Certainly I didn't know how to use the forge or a cutting torch when I started. I knew very little about ferrous metals, so I went through a period of intense investigation and then periods in which I thought about the process and did my other work. Then in late '69 I decided that if I was really going to do anything with the medium, I just had to stop doing anything else. Also at that time a book came out called *The Art of Blacksmithing* by Alex Bealer. Bealer was not a blacksmith. He ran an advertising agency and as a hobby he wrote books on traditional woodworking methods, so this was another book in his publication record. But he did have enough information that was of value for all of us. As a publicity thing concurrent with the publication of the book, he convinced the television newsman Charles Kuralt to do a small segment of the Kuralt program on blacksmithing—Alex brought together five old blacksmiths from Georgia, who commiserated about the death of blacksmithing and demonstrated the process. Anyway, we had a little bit of visiting artist

money, and I made a request for Bealer to do
a workshop.

Rick: So that was in . . . ?

Brent: Late April 1970 was when we had the workshop.
It was intended to be for my students' benefit, but
other metalsmiths heard about it and we ended up
having people come from as far as New York and
Colorado. Ultimately, seventy people showed up. A
new interest in blacksmithing emerged that week-
end, and some very well-established artists and metalsmiths who were here recognized that this medium
was going to be in the forefront of the crafts
movement. Most of the people who came to
Carbondale in 1970 were students and faculty
from other universities, and when they left they
went back to their studios and set up forges, so
there was a great deal of interest in the medium
from that point on. The film production unit at the
University found out about the workshop and
made an interesting documentary film of it about
fifty-nine minutes long.

Rick: So we still have the film then?

Brent: The University has a copy of it and I have a copy.
The American Crafts Council in New York City
paid part of the production costs on the film, and
it's available on a rental basis from them. In fact, I
showed it to my students last year. Anyway, in
1971 Alex Bealer called me and wanted to do
another conference/workshop. He asked me to be
the conference chairperson. He recommended a site
in Lumpkin, Georgia, and we had a second conference in '72 that was attended by another sixty or
seventy people. It was a very different group of
people at that time, many of them from the south-
east, very few students, very few educators. We fol-
lowed the next year with a second conference in

Cruciform

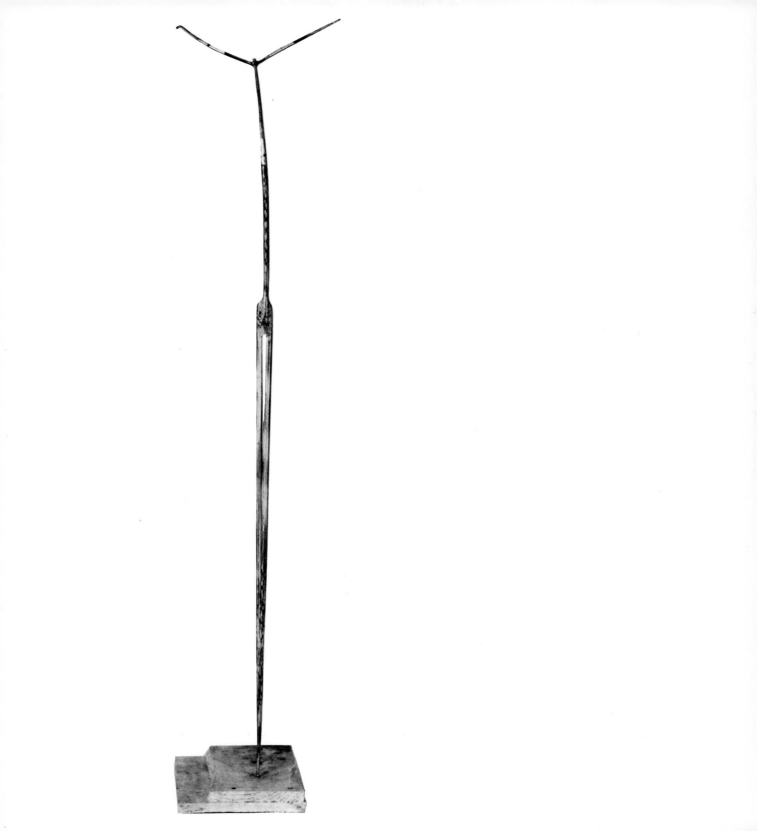

Lumpkin—maybe eighty people attended that time. The first Lumpkin conference really attracted a different audience than the Carbondale conference had. The second Lumpkin conference drew together a balance of people, those in education—students and faculty—and those who were active blacksmiths or just interested in smithing. As I recall, it was at the second Lumpkin conference that we decided we would establish an organization [ABANA, the Artist-Blacksmiths' Association of North America]. That would have been 1973. The following year the conference site was changed to Greenville, South Carolina. That drew 120 to 140 people. People with diverse interests and backgrounds came—neurologists, psychologists, and businessmen, as well as artist blacksmiths, people who probably had been messing around with their grandfather's forge or anvil, and some men like Judd Nelson, who had smithed all his life. And interest in the movement simply continued to grow.

In '74 we saw the bicentennial as an important event and as an opportunity to celebrate the blacksmith. By then I had a small facility at SIU and three graduate students studying blacksmithing. The students, because of their enthusiasm, suggested that the University host a conference and exhibition and try to have a major event. They talked me and Evert Johnson [curator of art for the University Museum] into the idea. Evert was very enthusiastic and wrote a number of grants to the NEA [National Endowment for the Arts] as well as to a lot of private corporations. He secured excellent funding. I think he ultimately received around eighty thousand dollars for an exhibition and conference. He planned the publication of the catalog, too. Anyway, the exhibition was considered significant enough that the American Crafts Museum asked to rent it for an opening in New York City, and the Renwick Gallery in Washington, D.C., also requested it. This was a show that was originally supposed to run for three months, and I think it was out almost a year.

Rick: So the American Crafts Museum took the material from the '76 show to New York?

Brent: Yes. Paul Smith was the director of the American Crafts Museum, and he served as a juror for the exhibition, which celebrated two hundred years of blacksmithing. The exhibition was essentially in two parts. There was a historical section and then there was current work, examples of ironwork that reflected what was happening in the field at that time. Paul and I were cojurors. He saw vitality and value in the selected historical pieces as well as in the contemporary work and thought it was important to take the show to New York. Then Lloyd Herman, the director of the Renwick Gallery in Washington, D.C., asked if he could arrange to have the show there. And this really took Evert aback because it created a different group of problems. Loan agreements for two to three months had to be extended. And how do you get the exhibition around? What are the additional costs, and how are they defrayed by the sites that are asking to take the exhibition on loan?

As for the conference itself, we thought it would be very good but strictly local. We thought we might attract maybe 250 people, which would be almost a doubling of the largest get-together. However, we had about 490 people attend. We had conferees from England, Italy, and practically every province in Canada. Someone showed up from almost every state in the United States. There are people that I've not seen since '76 who still refer to that conference. I was in England this summer, and an English blacksmith who had been here had just finished participating in a blacksmiths' conference. In fact, after he was here in 1976 he went back and started the British Artist-Blacksmiths' Association. He remarked that there would simply never be another conference like the one in '76. I had originally assumed that most blacksmiths were gone, but as this organization grew, it was like blacksmiths were coming out of the woodwork. Tom Bredlow out in Tucson, Arizona, a very quiet guy, had been making gates for the National Cathedral for a number of years, and at the '76 conference he did demonstrations and contributed a great deal. Frank Turley from Santa Fe, New Mexico, was an important participant, too—he teaches a six-week course in beginning blacksmithing, and I had sent students to study with him. So people had been working but had had very little communication with each other. There may have been some regional communication, but at the conference blacksmiths from across the U.S. were brought together and they recognized their need to communicate and to socialize. A brotherhood developed and ABANA became a national organization at that time. Today I think it has a recorded membership of well over three thousand. There are numerous regional organizations and state organizations now, and I'd think that the actual number of people working part- and full-time is much larger.

Rick: Nationally?

Brent: Yes. And I believe the British blacksmith organization has about three hundred members. Quite often when they have a conference, though, they attract blacksmiths from Europe—Czechoslovakia, France, Germany. Actually the press was quite remarkable in reporting the '76 Carbondale conference. United Press, the *Christian Science Monitor,* and other newspapers covered it; their articles ran in Japan, Korea, and all over Europe. The *St. Louis Post Dispatch* ran several color pages on us, and one of the Springfield newspapers did a big feature. All the articles were sent to the NEA, and they were obviously very pleased with the results of their funding.

So the impact of the conference was widespread. I just ran into somebody downtown recently who had been driving across Iowa and had come upon a kind of frontier village where a guy was working on the anvil. When the guy found out that my friend was from Carbondale, he explained that the '76 conference was the most important thing that had ever happened to him. Because of it, he had quit teaching high school English and had begun blacksmithing. A woman with a local travel agency called me up a year ago and said she had been in a remote part of Scotland. She said she had walked into a blacksmith's shop and had started chatting. When she told the blacksmith she was from Carbondale, Illinois, he said, "Oh, that's Southern Illinois University. Do you know Brent Kington?" So I get very interesting feedback. Evert Johnson and Jim Wallace, Bob Griffith, Joel Schwartz, and the other graduate students were all a part of something that was magic. My name gets associated with it, but it was really everybody pulling together.

The University recognized that something special had happened, too. They gave the blacksmithing program more support and applied for a Kresge grant, which was funded, so we got some extra tooling that we needed. As a result, the program today is the only master of fine arts program in blacksmithing in the United States. Well, it's a bachelor's program as well as a master's program. It's really the only degree-granting undergraduate-graduate program in the country, and the facilities are unquestionably the finest at any university in the United States. I get excellent applicants who want to study at SIU.

Rick: How many graduate students are in your program now?

Brent: I had eleven last year and I graduated six. I have eight right now.

Rick: Is it a two-year M.F.A.?

Brent: It's a two- to three-year M.F.A. program, depending on the student's effort.

Rick: How many undergraduates?

Brent: Oh, there must be around fourteen, not all in blacksmithing. We maintain a broad-based undergraduate and graduate metals program. The graduate students have a wide range of interests and personal directions—jewelers, enamelists, small object makers, blacksmiths. Right now, I have four blacksmiths. My colleague in the metalsmithing program is Richard Mawdsley, a very fine jeweler. We both feel it's important to keep a well-balanced program.

Rick: But you teach mainly the smithing part?

Brent: I'm in charge of the graduate program, and Richard is in charge of the undergraduate program. I work with jewelers as well as blacksmiths. I still do jewelry for my own personal interests, not for exhibition, but my preference is blacksmithing and I work with the blacksmithing students.

Rick: Can you tell me something about the kind of work you do now?

Brent: Yes. I'm primarily interested in wind-moving objects and kinetic sculpture. Most of my work deals with weather vanes and kinetic sculpture, moving pieces for the outside. I suppose there have been several influences on my work, certainly David Smith and Julio Gonzalez. Julio Gonzalez was one of the founders of Constructivism in sculpture; he was the first person to make sculpture by an additive process using space as an element. Prior to that, practically all sculpture was cast in bronze or cut out of stone or wood. He also introduced wrought iron and the oxygen-acetylene welding torch. Then after that museum experience at the Metropolitan, my most important reference points really became looking at ornamental ironwork, how iron has been used historically by people for tools, protection, arms, armor, instruments, and so forth. In 1973 I saw an exhibition of early American weather vanes and whirligigs at the American Folk Art Museum in New York, and I got very excited because I needed this idea for my own interests. I've always worked on the fringe of the crafts. I've never been interested in making coffee pots or serving silver or rings that fit people's fingers. The work I made through the sixties dealt with toys and precious metals, in part because they're not utilitarian. The weather vanes provide the same sort of freedom. I wouldn't be satisfied just making weather vanes that point in one direction. They have to do something else for me. I'm dealing with things that interest me that may or may not show accurate wind direction. They may just play in the wind. They may simply be a viewing experience, rather than an accurate instrument, although I can make a good weather vane if I want to. Also, I wasn't satisfied with the limitations of the traditional weather vane, which has a pin inside a post and the piece just turns on it. I'm into kinetic orchestrations. I deal not only with rotation but with pitch and yaw.

Rick: Can you tell me more about kinetic orchestration?

Brent: See this piece I've designed for the Botanical Gardens in Memphis, Tennessee? This is a mock-up; it's a 25 percent scale of what it's going to be.

Rick: You can play with it?

Brent: Oh yes, you can play with it. It has a little indentation with a point inside of it, and it gives me maximum flexibility as far as motion. And the addition of rods, which are really the sail of the weather vane, causes noise and light reflection and other motion so that when wind hits it, lots of things can happen.

Rick: Things you couldn't predict when you started doing it?

Brent: Yes.

Rick: So you get to discover, too.

Brent: Yes. And there's an element of challenge with these things that I find continually intriguing and kind of a puzzle to be resolved. When I do most of my pieces, I think of finding the balance point and what I relate it to is just a set of scales. If you put ten pennies on one side of the scale and ten on the other side, you're going to get a balance. This piece is like having a complex scale with three pans instead of two. So it's just a different type of exercise, one that I find interesting.

Rick: How long have you been working ·with the kinetic pieces?

Brent: Well, since 1973. I've been doing them going on fifteen years.

Weather Vane

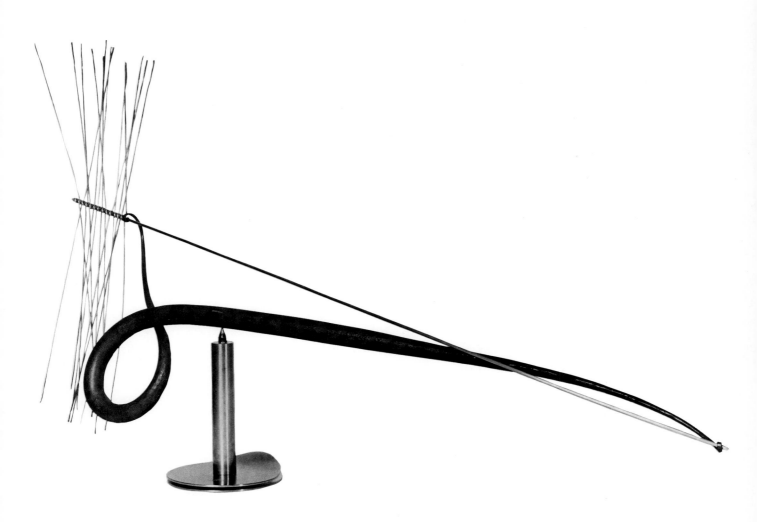

Rick: Do you find some of your students interested in them as well?

Brent: Not really, no. They have different directions and interests. I've got one student who's essentially making jewelry and containers; another person who's doing ornamental ironwork, beds, fireplace tools, benches, garden bench pieces; and a third who's doing sculpture as well as ornamental ironwork. Their work varies a great deal.

Rick: And you have a forge here at your home as well as on campus?

Brent: Yes, I have a forge up at the barn at the top of the hill, and this is really more of a thinking studio and a finishing studio. I do a lot of my own metal finishing and painting here.

Rick: You mean you paint the whirligigs and other things that move?

Brent: Yes. The piece up at the window, for instance, has been painted in acrylic, and there's another piece over on the ledge painted in acrylic. I use oil also. Actually, I do a lot of surface work. I've become increasingly interested in surface and in using it to extend my forms and express my ideas.

Rick: So the painting is less for preservation than it is for aesthetics?

Brent: Yes, it's more for content and aesthetics. I do paint for preservation, but it depends on what I'm doing. The big weather vane, the black one down there—that's painted essentially for preservation. That little orange piece down there has as much rust on it as there is paint. And of course stainless steel doesn't rust. So it depends on what my interests are and my intent.

Rick: But you put some kind of paint or finish on most of your work?

Brent: Most everything, yes.

Weather Vane

Rick: Can you clarify what you said before about your interest in the surface?

Brent: I find ferrous metal a very intriguing material. It's the most forgiving of all the metals that I've ever worked with other than high-karat gold. You can do anything with it. You can forge weld it, arc weld it, gas weld it, cut it in any number of ways. About the only thing you can do to it that's detrimental is to burn it. You can work it at temperatures all the way from high heat down to cold. It's very strong. You can do ornamental stamping on it while it's hot. With finishes, you can highlight the hammer marks to make them more visible. This little piece is a combination of rusted iron and painted iron, and the paint has been wiped or sanded through again. You'll notice that essentially it's an **X**-form but the way I've laid the paint, you get this tiny strange **V** that's dominant on the side. There's no other way I can attain that emphasis other than to paint it. Without the paint, it wouldn't have the same impact. I've tried to do the same thing with some of my weather vanes. There's a series of work that I did in 1981, a kinetic group. The basic content of these pieces is a mask image that reflects people's preoccupation with mysticism, theatre, and religion. Painting those pieces black wouldn't have helped me express that idea. I had to deal with surfaces and ornamented, spatial divisions. I didn't intend to replicate African, or pre-Columbian, or Iroquois, or Northwest Coast Indian work but simply to present my interpretation of people's involvement in areas of role playing or recognizing deity, throughout human history. That's what those pieces are about.

Rick: Do you do a lot of design work first?

Weather Vane

Brent: I think on paper in a shorthand way. If a particular line comes to my mind, I'll lay it down on paper, but I prefer to work with the metal. The process of forging is as much sketching as it is the direct process of making. And I play with it until I find exactly what I think is in my mind. I don't do a lot of formal drawing. I have drawing skills, and I may mess around quite a bit on paper, but then I go up to my shop and work directly with the material.

Rick: Can you tell me why you're in smithing?

Brent: I think it just suits me. It suits my aesthetic needs. There's certainly something very physical about the activity, and that feels good. I've always been a very physical person. I'm also a very direct person in what I do. I did casting for about a ten-year period, but as a process it's not immediate enough. Using traditional blacksmithing techniques is more immediate. You simply pick up a piece of metal, get it hot, and hit it, and you stop when you're done. There are no interim processes.

Rick: And you can see the effects immediately?

Brent: Sure, you can start and finish something. The hammer is the manipulation process; it's also the finishing process. It really suits my particular character in being physical and direct and bringing things to quick solutions or conclusions.

Rick: Was your grandfather a blacksmith? Was there someone early on who got you interested in blacksmithing?

Brent: No. I took a strange road getting here. My dad was a steam fitter and an excellent repairman and mechanic—which I've never been. He could rebuild car engines, electrical motors, and do lots of other things. I'm sure he despaired that I was never interested and didn't try. But no, I was just a

trained craftsman in precious metals, and I found
my way to another material and saw in it a wonderful potential, something I just couldn't resist
investigating. It's as simple as that.

Donald Asbee

Donald Asbee runs the Asbee Metal Studio *in Bland, Missouri, where this interview took place. He has practiced his trade for about twelve years doing both commission work and artistic pieces.*

Rick: Who got you started in blacksmithing?
Don: My roots in blacksmithing go back to horseshoeing school at Montana State University. After I dropped out of college, I had a wild hair to do something unusual. Never having been around horses didn't keep me from wanting to go to horseshoeing school. Once there, I learned the fundamentals of blacksmithing, as far as horseshoe making was concerned, and I also made various horseshoeing tools. I soon found that I was able to express myself in the metalwork involved with horseshoeing. That's what captivated me most about the trade.
Rick: Where were you going to college?
Don: Allegheny College in Meadeville, Pennsylvania. A lot of good people there. It's a small, liberal arts college, very personal—you knew everyone. If I'd wanted to learn, I could have, but I just closed it off because I couldn't figure out from one trimester to the next what I was going to do. After a year and a half in college, I didn't see any plan being formed. That was one of the hardest things, not having any direction. So I felt I needed to do something that would involve a commitment. Since I

liked working with my hands, I thought I'd go to horseshoeing school.

Somebody I knew, who had his degree in psychology, decided that he was going to chuck all the mind games associated with his business and go to horseshoeing school. This guy was kind of a role model to me—he was six or seven years older than I was—and here he was chucking a job at Princeton University to go to horseshoeing school. But even he didn't realize what he was doing. He thought he was going to become the village blacksmith. He was painting this idealistic picture for me, and I thought, well, now I have a reason to drop out of college. I told all my professors that I wasn't going to be around, and they thought I was doing the right thing. I was getting support from everybody at the time, except my dad was kind of upset about it.

Then I get a letter from Ken, the Princeton psychologist, who was already in horseshoeing school. He said, "Don, before you make any rash decisions, I want to tell you, this is not what I thought it was going to be. You're dealing with horses! They're unpredictable. It's very hard work, and we're having a real problem with the local people." Here's this eastern radical from Princeton, New Jersey, trying to shoe horses for ranchers in Montana. It was the first time folks out there had ever encountered a long-haired type. Well, I thought, I can't back out now—I'm committed. So before I went out to horseshoeing school, I cut my hair and then I arrived as Ken's friend. I found, though, that because there had been so much tension, the liberal types had made a real effort to get along with the conservative ranchers, and it turned out to be the most meaningful formal educational experience I'd had. I did better in horseshoeing school than I've ever done in any other formal training.

Rick: I know what blacksmithing school is like. You work like crazy, and you get burned, and you're around a bunch of other people who are getting burned. It's like running a gauntlet even if you don't have to deal with a lot of sociological differences.

Don: Yeah, that's right, but the sociological differences were dealt with properly, so it was really a good experience for me. But it wasn't until I got to horseshoeing school that I realized that I wasn't there to learn to be the village blacksmith. I'd gone all the way to Montana with fantasies of this romantic life of living in a little town and making everything for everybody.

Rick: And they'd stop in and everybody would be your pal.

Don: That's it, but I've still probably come close to that in creating the situation I have here.

Rick: A lot of younger blacksmiths I know were counter-culture types who wanted to do something with their hands, do something on their own.

Don: Yes, be beholden to no one.

Rick: Back to the land, the homesteader dream, get away from the cities.

Don: Yeah, that's an interesting point. That was my goal back when I was twenty.

Rick: You went to welding school, didn't you, Don?

Don: Yes, I did. I got into a CETA program in Bridge-ton, Missouri. My wife and I had to move up to St. Charles, Missouri, so that I'd be eligible. We'd been stuggling out here in Bland for two or three years. It'd been incredible just trying to build a horseshoeing business when you didn't know anybody, and you didn't know how to get along with

people in a rural area. I'd tried a lot of odd jobs in order to keep things going between horses. I worked as a small engine mechanic at the MFA [Missouri Farmers' Association] Co-op, and I had a real interesting job for about a year doing the blasting for a mining concern. It was hard physical labor, and it wasn't a secure job because of the weather, but I enjoyed it. Then I got laid off, and I realized that I didn't want to go through life just doing part-time things. Horseshoeing didn't seem like it was going anywhere at that point, and since I did like metalwork, I decided that I needed some formal training.

Having been laid off, I was able to get into this welding school program. I was probably one of the only students in class who had any intention of using the training. A lot of people involved in those programs were killing time. The instructors would put you in a welding practice booth, give you a pile of electrodes, and say, "Make beads on these little pieces of scrap plate. Weld little pieces of plate together." You didn't learn anything about welding design. They just wanted to keep you busy. But the experience of learning how to run a bead was important. From there, I got into a manpower program that involved building custom trailers in Wentzville, Missouri, and that was where I really put all my metalworking skills to work.

Rick: You got some on-the-job training.

Don: Yeah. I worked at that shop—it was a small outfit—for about seven months, and the guy I worked for was not keen on actually designing. He'd put something down on paper in general terms and say, "Okay it's up to you guys to figure out," and that gave me an opportunity to show some imagination in approaching design problems. While I look back at my efforts as rather crude, it was definitely a good learning experience. I built a lot of trailers with the help of the other people on the crew. There were about five or six of us, and we'd have about three different trailers going at a time, usually all different. I built a really large trailer that was eventually outfitted with a concrete batch plant and taken up to the Alaska pipeline.

Rick: A heavy-duty trailer.

Don: Yeah, so there were a lot of challenges, and I think that really gave me confidence.

After having been in the St. Charles area for a couple of years learning and working, I figured it was time to quit the job in Wentzville and move back out to Bland to open up my shop. I'd saved enough money working so I was able to make a commitment and build a shop and start from there. Then I met a fellow by the name of Jim Spralls about a month after I opened the shop. He was a horseshoer from California. He stopped in one day out of the blue and wanted to know where I was getting coal. I was messing around. I didn't know anything about blacksmithing other than making horseshoes and pokers and stuff. Jim was at the same point, too. He'd been into horseshoeing pretty heavily, but as far as actual blacksmithing went, he didn't know a whole lot more than I did. We really fed on each other's energy. Jim introduced me to ABANA [the Artist-Blacksmiths' Association of North America]. That was the point at which I decided that my work was going to be decorative ironwork. I built the shop mostly as a place to work on rainy days when shoeing wasn't practical, and I soon realized that it was the metalwork that was really going to hold my interest. A couple of years after opening the shop, I discontinued

horseshoeing because it wasn't what I wanted to do. Let me see if I can put this into words. The horses were a little too unpredictable, and I like predictability. Not that metalwork is totally predictable, but you have a lot more control than you do with horses.

Rick: Steel is a homogeneous substance. Horses aren't homogeneous.

Don: That's right. I felt that I'd started doing what I wanted to do when I stopped shoeing horses and concentrated solely on the ironwork. From there, the first workshop I attended was the Eric Moebius and Tom Bredlow symposium over at SIU, Edwardsville. When I saw what was going on there, it brought everything together for me. Another thing that influenced me was the Dona Meilach book, *Decorative and Sculptural Ironwork*. I started reading it about the same time I went to that workshop. Originally, before I even went to horseshoeing school, I'd gotten ahold of Alex Bealer's book, *The Art of Blacksmithing*.

Rick: I was at that workshop too. It legitimized blacksmithing and made me feel that it might be possible to make a living at it.

Don: That's it. Joan, my wife, and I went nine years without having any children, and money was really secondary. But then we realized that we had to create a little more security as time went by.

Rick: Because of your family?

Don: Yeah. The family is really important. I've got to learn how to make a living. I have to set some financial priorities. And so even though I haven't done very well financially up to this point, I think if I can attain in twelve or thirteen years what was a mere fantasy at twenty, I can probably make smithing pay off as time goes by.

Whale Vane

Rick: What are you currently working on? Could you describe that for me a little, please?

Don: Yes. I'm building forged and fabricated steel signs for the new headquarters building that the Kellogg Company is building in Battle Creek, Michigan—five signs that will be approximately fifty-five feet long.

Rick: So you're starting to get corporate architectural commissions?

Don: That's right.

Rick: What other types of work have you been doing?

Don: I started out doing farm equipment repair, but I've built many different kinds of furnaces and fireplace doors, fireplace inserts, fireplace parts, fireplace tools, stoves, and a lot of different designs in free-standing wood stoves. I've concentrated these past seven or eight years on wood-heating equipment, and I've made a reputation at it.

Rick: That's timely. People have been interested in saving money on their heating bills, and the cost of natural gas has been steadily rising, and you live in an area with a lot of forests. It seems like a good product.

Don: It worked out really well. I started making fireplace stoves that can convert your fireplace into a highly efficient heat source for your home. I built my first one back in 1977, and they were basically unheard of before that in this area. As time went on, within three years, I was the one to contact, and then before too long, the mass production people came into the market.

Rick: They caught up with you.

Don: Yes. That was a learning experience for me. My best year, I sold close to fifty stoves. I was just working all the time—it was terrific. So I took all my working capital and put it into twenty thou-

sand pounds of one-quarter-inch steel plate. Then we decided to have kids, and the next year we had a little baby, and I probably built less than twenty stoves that year. All of a sudden, there was a new wood stove company opening up every week, it seemed like. Then before long the market was glutted, and it was a "market adjust" for the next couple of years. I hadn't concentrated on diversification, and it was a rude awakening. But except for the investment in steel plate, I hadn't committed myself heavily to specialized equipment for stove making. I'd considered doing a small-scale factory operation—a shear, a brake, and that kind of stuff—and really becoming production oriented, making one or two styles. I'm really glad I didn't do that.

Once I'd made a name for myself in wood stoves, I started concentrating on expensive stoves that nobody could get on a mass-produced basis. I went after the top 5 percent of the market. The mass-produced units wouldn't be able to satisfy those people's needs. And they knew that they'd have to spend more money on what they wanted. I figured my blacksmithing abilities enabled me to set my work apart from what was on the market.

Rick: Because you could put forged decorative elements on your stoves and differentiate them from the ones that didn't have that?

Don: That's right. The designs fit. I know that a lot of the stuff I built back then is kind of funky, but at least I was making the hardware to match the overall design of the stove. People liked the idea that, if they were willing to spend the money, they could come into my shop and talk to me. I could show them my portfolio, and then I'd go to their

house and look at the architecture of the home and the way the furniture was arranged and build all of that into the stove. I wouldn't even attach the door handles to the stove until I knew where the stove was going.

Rick: There's a good point here. The flexibility that blacksmiths have is to their advantage. If the market floods in one certain area, they can shift to other areas. That's always been a strong point for blacksmiths through the five- or six-thousand-year history of blacksmithing. If the war stops and the sword business goes down, they can start on plowshares.

Don: That's right. You don't have too much tied up in specialized capital equipment. You're using the same anvil that you made stove handles on, but now you're starting to make balustrades for your architectural business. You're dealing with very fundamental techniques that are applicable to a broad range of items. The reaction to a changing market can be very quick. All it really takes is just changing your mind. It really broke me up that I wasn't going to be able to make stoves anymore. Then I realized I still have my shop. I don't have to change much, just continually streamline my operation. The most critical thing is to concentrate on markets that aren't flooded. Look for the demand. Find out who's out there looking for something they can't get.

Rick: And look for markets that are small, that the mass producer won't mess with.

Don: Exactly. It's great to know how to forge and how to mortise and tenon. Those are fine disciplines. They fit in nicely with various designs, and they're wonderful, but that isn't being a blacksmith, necessarily. You have to produce.

Rick: There's a lot of hard physical work involved in blacksmithing as well as a lot of creativity and mental exercise. Can you try to tell me why you wanted to do this, Don?

Don: There's something about steel, ferrous metals. They have a special characteristic. Francis Whitaker [a leading artist blacksmith] put it most succinctly when he pointed out that steel is a stubborn material. To be able to gain mastery over something stubborn, you yourself have to be a lot more stubborn than the material. At any point, you're either dealing with mental gymnastics or the gymnastics that can be seen when you're working efficiently at the anvil. You're not just beating something. You choreograph your efforts so that you're able to effectively influence the material that you're working with. I don't care whether it's forge work or fabrication. I think that fabrication can require just as much mental and physical stamina. There's just something to be said for taking a piece of steel and fashioning it into something else that has a totally different character than the material you started with.

It's a challenge and a channel for expression. I've tried working in wood, and probably, if I'd had a good teacher in wood, I could have learned to appreciate it. You can do a lot of things with wood that you can do with metal when it comes to building things, but I much prefer ferrous metal. It's the medium that works for me. And I feel I'm just scratching the surface. I hope I can consider myself a master someday, but I definitely don't consider myself a master now even though I've done some nice things. I look at them as practice pieces. And there are a lot of things that I want to do.

Rick:　What are they? What are your goals in blacksmithing?

Don:　Architectural work. I wouldn't even hesitate to do structural steel work in a building. In fact, my goal now is to build a home, hopefully within the next few years, a home that will be built of structural steel, the way a construction company would build a professional building or a skyscraper. I want to build it using the same techniques. I like to weld and have already started working on blueprints for the preliminary floor plan and what not. I'm going to pick the minds of the architects and everybody involved in this type of construction. I want to make sure that what I build is correct and acceptable.

But I think that structural ironwork is satisfying even if you're just doing a patio deck for somebody. I've done that kind of work and I like it. Another thing that would be fun would be to work on a project like the St. Louis Arch or the Statue of Liberty, some large-scale project where you're working with a bunch of different people from all over the world. I think even though you might be doing something rather mundane like fillet welds, there would still be so much to be gained by having participated in a project like that. Obviously, it'd be a lot of fun to have something important to do on a piece that would be of national or international stature. That's kind of an ultimate goal.

*R*obert Schantz

Robert Schantz is a diversified, suburban blacksmith who has been practicing for approximately eleven years. The interview took place at his shop, the Spanish Lake Blacksmith Shop, on Bellefontaine Road in St. Louis County, Missouri.

Rick: Bob, could you tell me a little about how you got started in blacksmithing?

Bob: Well, I moved to a farm in Tennessee in 1974 and built a small shop and began experimenting on my own. Then in 1975 I went to horseshoeing school in Memphis. I tried to plan it. I intentionally moved to Tennessee because a horseshoeing school was there and because I could buy property for next to nothing. We had a two-year plan. We'd move down, and I'd spend those two years trying to get as much information and skill as I could, and then we'd move back to this area. I did that deliberately because I felt that when I came back, I'd be new to the customers but somewhat experienced as a blacksmith.

Rick: Before you had training in Memphis, what was your shop like?

Bob: I had Alex Bealer's book [*The Art of Blacksmithing*], as many of us did, and I experimented from there. I learned a lot of mistakes from Bealer's book. I thought it was a good book—I'm not saying it wasn't—but it was the only book that I could find at the time.

Rick: He was pioneering. He helped start the renaissance in blacksmithing in the United States with that book.

Bob: He at least got us all thinking about it again and searching. If his answers or suggestions were wrong, at least he was searching for the right ones.

So, anyway, I built a wooden forge with a duck's nest [the part of the forge that contains the fire] and a hearth lined with clay. The duck's nest was a little too deep and didn't work all that well. I could get a terrific amount of smoke with very little fire. Of course, I couldn't get a piece hot except on the tip unless I'd bend it in half, so that was disastrous. But I learned that I needed to go to somebody who had already gone through the errors and have them teach me.

Rick: We didn't really have too many people around in those days to teach us. It wasn't like you could walk into a shop and say, "I'd like to apprentice here—I'd like to learn the blacksmith's trade," as you could if you wanted to be, say, a pipe fitter or a welder.

Bob: As a matter of fact, when I bought my anvil from Rudy Williams [see part 1] in '72 and I tried teaching myself, I had to reinvent the wheel a few times. In Tennessee, there were two older blacksmiths, and they'd talk forever to you and they were as friendly as could be, but they wouldn't tell you anything or show you anything. I talked to several people, primarily welders, and told them I wanted to learn about blacksmithing. They all had the same comment phrased in different words, "Well, there's nothing to it. You just heat the steel and beat it until it gets to the state that you want." Then I began thinking I was clumsy because if all you had to do was heat it and beat it until it got

into the proper shape, I'd better get a job sitting at a desk.

Rick: Which shoeing school did you go to?

Bob: Midsouth Academy of Horseshoeing just outside of Memphis. We did a lot of work in the fire. Some of the first tools I made were pretty bad—they ended up in the trash heap—but I guess that's the only way you learn a trade or craft. And I learned a lot at horseshoeing school about forge work, fortunately.

Rick: After you got out of shoeing school, you went back to St. Louis?

Bob: No. I worked another year down there shoeing horses and doing what little blacksmithing I was able to do. But that wasn't for pay. That was just learning, weekends and evenings. The first year after I got out of school, my work was experimental.

Tony Ranciglio in St. Louis helped me the most in blacksmithing. I might have tried to pick something up from the others I talked to, but I spent time in his shop, and he showed me and told me why and how.

Rick: So he was the mentor figure in your life?

Bob: Yeah. He fit the pattern pretty well. He'd been a city blacksmith for about thirty years. He was colorful and fit your image of an old blacksmith.

Rick: What kind of business did Tony do?

Bob: All tool work. Just sharpening and making rakers, ripper points, moil points [jackhammer points], that sort of thing. I'd sharpen a moil point and get it too hard a couple inches back. It'd break and I'd apologize and redo it. Tony would have that happen, and he'd throw it down and cuss the guy out that brought it in and tell him that the guy who'd

Horseshoeing trailer

used the jackhammer didn't know how to use it right. And he got by with it. Had I done that, I think they would have gone to somebody else to get the work done. I took some of my broken points to Tony to see what I was doing wrong, but he said it was the operator. Well, I haven't had any breaks since, but then I changed the way I do it. So I didn't really have a formal training program for blacksmithing. I had no one other than Tony Ranciglio. I went to seminars, clinics, and conferences. I read a lot and I learned from working by trial and error.

Rick: Trial and error isn't so bad in a blacksmith shop. If you've got a general idea of what's going on, you can make a few quick studies of a forging process and figure it out if it isn't too elaborate.

Bob: The trial and error method is much faster for me now. I make fewer errors than I did before.

Rick: Becoming a competent smith takes about ten years. I guess if you were the son of a blacksmith and were apprenticed when you were a kid, maybe you wouldn't have to go through that much time, but for people just starting from scratch, I think ten years is a good figure.

Bob: I would think so. When I got out of horseshoeing school, I thought I knew everything about horses and horseshoeing, but now I think even in that field, which is sort of an offshoot of blacksmithing, you need a good five years before you really know how to shoe a horse properly.

Rick: You have a master's degree, don't you? In what?

Bob: Theology. My educational background didn't prepare me at all for what I ended up doing. My bachelor's degree was in sociology, and now I'm confronted with math problems, art problems, and business management problems, and so I learn by my mistakes in these areas, too. That's costly as well as frustrating.

Rick: As I look around your shop, there's horseshoeing equipment and horseshoes, nippers, alligator clinchers, and hammer handles—like a salesroom.

Bob: I sell retail to local horseshoers, so we've got a retail supply store for those folks. I shoe very few horses now, but I still do some in the immediate area. Most farriers in the country now have a large area that they travel to. I've cut back quite a bit on the shoeing. I just do retail sales and manufacture a portable gas forge.

Rick: What's the name of that forge?

Bob: Forge Master. I got a patent on it last year, and it's selling pretty well because it operates with no blower. It operates on a Venturi principle and heats up a shoe or a pair of shoes or whatever you put in it in about three minutes. For a horseshoer, he can pull up, bring the horse out, throw its shoes in, and by the time he's got one or two feet trimmed, the shoes are ready to work. Most people in barns aren't opposed to a gas forge, but coal smoke and sparks scare them, so it's a much more efficient forge for field use. It has limitations, so here at the shop, I use coal and gas. On some jobs, it's more efficient to use gas, and on other jobs, more efficient to use coal. I think this year I'm going to build a different case for the forge which would allow long pieces to be slid through. I think some fabricators or ornamental smiths that are doing production runs may be interested in it. You can stack many pieces in it. I do all my moil points in that forge. I've recently gotten it running on natural gas, which has a couple of benefits. It's a little more economical than propane; it's convenient. It also burns less scale. I think the reason is that I

had to open the orifice up, so the same amount of air is drawn in but more gas burns with the oxygen. With propane, you get more scale than with coal because that oxygen is blasting right on the metal. With natural gas, you still get a little more scale than with coal but quite a bit less than with propane.

Rick: What kind of heats do you get out of it?

Bob: You can weld in it, so you get twenty-three or twenty-four hundred degrees Fahrenheit.

Rick: And you do a lot of tool work in your shop for your fellow horseshoers and other people, too?

Bob: Well, I make fore punches for punching the nail head set in the horseshoe and pritchels for clearing out the nail hole. I ship those to probably thirty dealers around the country, and the farrier supply stores sell them.

Rick: What's your brand name?

Bob: Anvil brand.

Rick: That keeps you busy here, and then you get walk-in business?

Bob: You get contractors for sharpening moil points or rakers for tuck-pointers and that sort of thing. And then occasionally, three or four times a year, a company will need some special tool or part fabricated or forged, and so I do those.

Rick: This seems like a good location for a shop in that you have a lot of business exposure from people just walking and driving by all the time.

Bob: Most of the time that's a plus; sometimes it's a minus. You get a lot of people when you're in the middle of forging who stop in and want to talk or have you explain something about blacksmithing. It's hard to be rude, but as you know, you can't just leave a piece sitting in the fire forever.

Rick: You do any ornamental work?

Bob: Yeah. I don't feel really confident with ornamental work. I've done some porch railings. I feel good when I'm done with them, and I'm not ashamed of the pieces, but the problem is that they're not cost effective for me because I take too long. I've stopped doing repair welding because you can't make much money at it. I'm not greedy, but I can't spend too much time charging a little bit of money for something. And people will bring in a shovel that's completely broken in two, and it'll take an hour to weld it up, and they could buy a new shovel for twelve dollars. There's a retired fellow around the corner that I send all the welding to. That works out best for both of us.

Rick: This is a historic building you're working in, isn't it, Bob?

Bob: Yeah, it was built in 1875 as a blacksmith shop. The fellow who built it—his name was Jake Wilhelm—was an ironworker. He moved out to Spanish Lake and built the original shop across the street. He ran that for two years and then built this shop. It was the first business in this section of Spanish Lake.

Spanish Lake was the recreational area for the French and Spanish troops. It was settled in 1720, I think they said. When the Spanish first began using it, Bellefontaine Road used to be called Plank Road because from the city limits out to here, it was literally a wooden road. They just laid planks across the dirt to keep it so people could travel even during muddy times.

Rick: Do you like the physicality of blacksmith work?

Bob: Oh yeah. There are some things I don't like about the shop. I would much rather have a little bit larger, cleaner shop, but I don't like sitting at a

Working at anvil with Forge Master in background (right)

Rick: desk. I had that for a while. I enjoy the physical work.

Rick: You could have done a lot of other things. You had educational opportunities. Why work in a blacksmith shop?

Bob: In 1972, I was interested theoretically in blacksmithing because it just seemed intriguing. But in '72 I also bought part interest in a racehorse. I really enjoyed animals, especially horses. I didn't want to be a trainer, a jockey was obviously out of the question, and that left horseshoeing, which tied in with my hobby interest in blacksmithing. My dad was a carpenter and loved working wood. I enjoyed working by myself and working with my hands. When I realized that blacksmithing requires that you work with your mind probably more than with your hands, I figured that I needed a lot longer time to learn it than I had initially thought. At the time, I had a wife and son—I still do—so I didn't really think I'd be able to get into it full-time because of responsibilities. We decided to just try it. We could always go broke and find something else to do.

I tried it and I really do like it. I don't think I could do anything else now. There are days when if somebody walked in, I'd give them the whole business and other days when there wouldn't be enough money to buy it. I guess that's true with anybody who's in business for themselves, but with this one I've got some release for anxieties. It's therapeutic because if I get stress-filled from any kind of situation, whether it's business or personal or whatever, I can work in the shop for an hour, and it's as relaxing as some other form of therapy. I can always stop doing one thing and move on to something different. It's interesting, enjoyable, and relaxing all at once.

I used to be very excitable and quick tempered, but I've changed. It takes an awful lot for me to get angry now, and I think one of the reasons is because to do forge work properly, you can't be rushed and hurried and easily excitable. I think to do it right, you have to be calm. Tony Ranciglio taught me that the first time he taught me hardening and tempering. He liked to drink beer. He'd forge a piece of steel, heat it back up, and then set it to the side to normalize. He'd say, "Now we gotta go in the house and have a beer. It's timed just right. When we finish the beer, then we harden the steel." So we'd go in and have a beer. Before I did much blacksmithing I'd want to get steel normalized right now, and then harden and temper right now. But steel just doesn't work that way, and so it forces you to be a little more patient and a little more relaxed.

Also to me there's a mystique or magic involved. In a forge weld, for example, I put two pieces of metal in the fire, and if I do the proper blessings and incantations, I can hammer them together. And with luck, you can't see where they were hammered together. There are very few mediums that you can do that with, and to me, that's sort of magical. I'm still awed by it.

*T*homas Gipe

*T*homas *Gipe,* *a professor in the Department of Art and Design at Southern Illinois University, Edwardsville, has been a sculptor and artist blacksmith for nearly eleven years. He was interviewed at his home outside Edwardsville, Illinois.*

Rick: You're a sculpture professor, but you teach black-smithing and you frequently employ blacksmithing techniques. Is that right?

Tom: Yes. When I used to go to blacksmithing conventions, it bothered me a little bit. I don't use pure blacksmithing techniques. I cast iron and bronze. Nearly all my pieces have some wood elements in them. By the way, I certainly don't call myself a bronze caster although I'm a mold maker, and I certainly don't call myself a woodworker. Some of the wood things I even hire out. I know cast iron fairly well, but I'm not an expert.

Rick: Do you define yourself as a blacksmith?

Tom: Yes, I do. That hasn't always been true, but in the last few years, I think I can honestly call myself a blacksmith. I thought about that a lot in conjunction with blacksmiths who make a living black-smithing, and I justified calling myself a blacksmith because of having the ability or the opportunity to do research. I've been very directly influenced by my university research grants. I've been here eleven years, and I've had one every year. The university in its benevolence forces me to be accountable, and

I think it's good in that I've had to make a continuum through all these different research grants, which are usually for a three-year period. Basically, I had to start planning my research eleven years ago. And by doing research, I guess I've learned a lot of things that perhaps even some of my friends who are commercial blacksmiths don't have an opportunity to do, like fiddling around making Damascus [patterned] steel or taking hours to do something. If you were doing a gate and some customer wanted it, you wouldn't do that.

Rick: Who got you started in this? When I ask that, Tom, I'm trying to get the early influences on you, early imagery. I know your grandfather was a blacksmith.

Tom: Yes. As a matter of fact, as a kid I used to spend Saturdays working with him. He was a tough task master. It seemed like everything I tried to do was wrong, and of course, looking back on it, it was. But as a kid, you get real sensitive to things like that. You think you're not doing a good job. I think it influenced me in a way that's stronger than I might have imagined at the time, because I spent ten years after my B.A. in college—I had no art training—in advertising. Then I took some art hours at the University of Nebraska. I started as a fabricator, a welder, a sculptor. I had a fine undergraduate instructor, Sidney Buchanan, who was a very narrow person as a sculptor in terms of the materials he used, not as an artist. But he welded and I thought that was how you made sculpture, and I stuck with that thinking through graduate school. I also began doing a little bit of bronze casting. It was all self-taught.

Then I got my first job in Minnesota, teaching, and I began to draw on early images from my life

Hofman's Smithing Magician Number One

on the farm as subject matter in my drawing and sculpture. When I moved to Minnesota, my grandfather had died and my dad—I was down visiting him—said, "You know, there are some tools your grandfather had. You ought to get them." So I took my grandfather's anvil and some tongs, but I left his beautiful forge. At that stage, I was working everything cold—that was the way I'd been trained—but I began to realize the limitations of that. When you bend something, it would split or break, and then I thought, well, of course, blacksmiths heat the metal up to bend it. I would heat the metal with an acetylene torch and do some trial pieces, which frankly didn't fit into my work directly. Then my father passed away and my mother said, "You'd better get the tools out of here. We're selling everything." So I went over there and loaded up this old twenty-five-pound, Caryhard power hammer. I had no idea what a Little Giant was at the time or even what the Caryhard was. I do remember it running when I was a kid—the shop filled with smoke, my grandfather drawing out plowshares—and after I got it loaded, this guy who'd been my dad's hired man for forty years said, "Let's load this forge up, too." So I took it, not realizing that it was really a gem of a forge, in perfect condition, no cracks or anything, a cast-iron Buffalo forge.

So I brought the thing down to Edwardsville and set it up and began doing some blacksmith work. It was just a nightmare, a disaster. I'd swing the hammer and hit the anvil. I'd hit the work piece when it was too cold. I'd just beat on the stuff. I thought about giving up several times. Doing it alone was an incredible frustration, making these hideous things and not being able to

Hammering out a Damascus billet

imagine in my wildest dreams that they could be used for anything. Even visually, they couldn't be used. But I had to say to myself, you spent all this time getting this tooling together—you can't give up.

Rick: Who were the other people who influenced you?

Tom: I think probably, like a lot of people, I was influenced by the famous Carbondale ABANA [Artist-Blacksmiths' Association of North America] convention. A lot of people commented that there will never be another convention like the 1976 Carbondale convention, and I agree with that because of the timing. Everybody showed up; nobody knows why. I saw Tom Bredlow and Francis Whitaker working. I met Eric Moebius, Emmert Studebaker, Brent Kington [see part 5], Daryl Meier [see part 4], Al Paley, and anybody who happens to be anybody in this business. They were all there, but many of these people weren't recognized. Hardly anybody knew Francis at that time. Eric Moebius was a young kid. A few people knew who Bredlow was. The atmosphere was just wonderful. The seventies was such an open time, too. Everything seemed possible. And to me, it was infectious, but I had this problem. No one I knew about was making sculpture using blacksmithing techniques except Brent Kington. And it's easy enough to say you're going to start making sculpture as a blacksmith, but it's much harder to do.

Rick: You worked with Francis Whitaker, didn't you?

Tom: As I said, I met him down at the Carbondale convention in 1976. I was just another guy bugging him. Everybody was. They all wanted to stand next to him and to have his knowledge by osmosis. He wrote in a note to the *Anvil's Ring,* which was just a little newsletter then, that he would do

workshops, so I sent him an airmail, special delivery letter that same day that said, "Well, you can do one for me." Francis is a very efficient man, and I think the whole transaction took place in about a week. I got a letter back and Francis said, "I'll be there at these dates," and that was how I began my relationship with him. I'm sure he must have just cringed when he saw the eight or ten of us sitting around. He said, "Well, what do you want to see?," and we said, "Well, we don't know anything and we want to see everything."

He came back a time or two, and I had gotten a sabbatical leave and was talking about going to Europe to do research when Francis said, "Why don't you come to the Mountain Forge in Aspen, Colorado?" So we worked out all the incidentals, and I went out there and spent a summer working with him, which was the turning point for me. He taught me how to forge weld. I had fiddled around, as every blacksmith does, with welding. Sometimes the pieces would stick; sometimes they wouldn't. If anything, he taught me that and also how to conceptualize the piece we were forging. So it was exactly what I needed because for the life of me I couldn't figure out how to make sculpture using blacksmithing. My first attempts were some traditional things, little gates and fences, that sort of thing. That summer with Francis Whitaker came at a good time because I was just on the periphery of smithing, beating on some hot iron. I'm not sure I learned much in Aspen because I was so green and there just wasn't time to learn that much, but I saw things that I would remember years later. Now I know why he did something a certain way. I didn't understand then, but now I do. Unfortunately, not many people have an opportunity, except at SIU, Carbondale, to work with a really terrific blacksmith. You can learn it on your own, but it's much easier not to. I decided I was going to have to learn the traditional skills first because I didn't want to do a bunch of smash and bash. (There's a term for it now, but there wasn't then.) So I became determined to start at the bottom.

Rick: To get control of the material?

Tom: Yes. To get the tools under control and to learn everything I possibly could about fires. Of course, blacksmith tools were everywhere around here a few years ago. You can still find them but not with the regularity that you could ten years ago. There were junkyards with piles of anvils and post vices. I used to pick up a lot of tools at yard sales in Edwardsville because people didn't know what they were. People thought a top swage was some kind of weird hammer. And the stuff was not only easy to find but cheap, in some cases more than cheap. Some people would say, "You can have it," because it was just sitting in their yard. But the days of those fifty- and seventy-five-dollar power hammers are obviously gone forever now. Anyway, I have the same feeling about tools as collectors of antique automobiles have about cars.

Rick: You like to collect tools?

Tom: Yes. I enjoy the tools in and of themselves. I restored them and found out how they worked, and then a strange thing began to happen. Not only anvils but just about every tool I ran into fascinated me. Old blacksmiths knew why they were shaped the way they were, but I didn't. It was a mystery. So even though I was getting nowhere, I became intrigued with the tools themselves and their design, form, and function.

　　I've seen an anvil or two that were probably as

near perfect, design-wise, as anything I've ever seen. I saw one when Brent [Kington; see part 5] had the U.S. Solid Wrought Show in Carbondale in 1976. I interpreted it to be an American-made anvil by its design. It was a two-hundred pounder, and I'm sure it was in pristine condition. I don't know the brand name. I looked at that anvil for fifteen or twenty minutes. I walked around it and I thought, this is a piece of sculpture, a gorgeous piece of sculpture, aside from the fact it's a functional tool. Probably that influenced me more than the work of Albert Paley and some of the other famous artists like Tom Bredlow, Francis Whitaker, Jim Wallace, and Brent Kington. I admire and respect all those people's work, but there was something mysterious about that anvil. The makers were probably long dead, and the factory that made it probably wasn't even around anymore. I had always wondered what working next to a two-hundred pound piece of metal at a welding heat would be like, and I truly believe that my inspiration to do blacksmithing stemmed from seeing that incredible anvil. One of my students, Bruce McCoy, had nearly the same experience as I did looking at that anvil, but I didn't find out about it until years later. I had another graduate student who used to talk about my quest for the perfect anvil, which I'll never find. I have numerous anvils and have repaired them, but now I've gotten so damn picky I won't buy anything that needs to be repaired.

Anyway, as an artist, I went through a period of feeling guilty around all the conceptual artists. I used to be kind of a closet technician because I didn't want people to know how much I enjoyed tools. When you had your shop over in St. Louis, I remember you saying, Rick, that the tools were your friends, and it really stuck with me because I thought it was such a curious comment. But then I realized that I gain a lot of gratification from the tools. I thought, well, of course, you damn fool, this is where your ideas are coming from, and I was ignoring that fact because I felt guilty about it. After all, in the world of art at the time, you weren't supposed to be a technician. It was out of fashion. Finally I got to the point where I didn't care about fashion because I don't sell sculpture and I don't have to sell gates. I'm a research blacksmith, a research artist. I don't need to worry about selling because the state pays me a salary as a university professor. But this understanding unfolded slowly. It took me three or four years to finally get the courage to make a piece of sculpture with a hammer in it because I love the shape of a hammer or to make a piece of sculpture with my version of a hot cutter in it. When I actually began to figuratively design blacksmithing tools into my sculpture, I really enjoyed it, although I'd never dreamed that the tools would actually influence or inspire my sculpture, my work. And there was this—I guess I have to be kind of corny about it— joyful sort of benefit to seeing these tools as they really were intended.

I sometimes buy tools these days that I don't need just because I like the way they look. I like what the hammer looks like when it gets a polish on it, when you get a polish on your anvil. I like to see the polish on the edge of the forge where your hand always puts the tongs down, the polish on the handles of your fire tools. The hand-forged tools mean more to me than they used to. I didn't used to know the difference. You know, a lot of the stuff is drop-forged. Probably most of my tools now are drop-forged, but when I find a handmade tool made by a blacksmith, I buy it and I wish that I'd have done more of that.

Rick: Do you like the physicality of blacksmithing?

Tom: Very much so. Back again to this business of having to be embarrassed because I'm technically involved in my work, a secret technician. I also began to realize that the simple quality of moving the metal around really is what sculpture is about. I don't mean to be an art historian here, but in the twentieth century we do things backwards as sculptors. We fabricate pieces from things that are already made. The mill turns out a sheet of steel or an I-beam and we cut things and put them together, but the old idea of sculpture was to take a piece of stone or wood or a piece of wax and to mold something or remove material. I've thought a lot about how I was missing something as an artist because I had learned the new way of doing things but not the old way. It was like learning blacksmithing traditionally before I began to make sculpture with it. I wanted to do that because I didn't want to miss something. I realized looking at this metal move around that the metal was plastic exactly as wax is plastic, and as a sculptor, I had to react to that.

And now I feel just wonderful about my work. I could be shut in a room with my blacksmith tools, and I'd never run out of ideas for sculpture. What a pleasant thing for an artist. So it was just a question of getting in tune with myself. There was a lot that all added together—remembering my grandfather's wonderful shop, the belts flapping, and the line shafts and the smoke everywhere, and the farmers on the rainy days with the trucks com-

Tressa's Anvil Dance

ing over to get things fixed; the Carbondale convention; the time with Francis; the inspiration of seeing certain tools and collecting some tools.

Rick: Tell me about your work now.

Tom: I do some Damascus things now. I do representations of tools. I'll forge out a pair of tongs that's going to be used decoratively. I'll forge a small hammer that's in a piece of sculpture. Certain things that would drive you nuts trying to forge them—organic things like a pig's head—I cast. Being a sculptor, I like the process, the technical side of making things.

My sculpture is made in human terms. I don't build gigantic commercial sculpture. My work is very personal, very much on a human scale. I like my sculpture to have the same kind of polish that the edge of the forge has or the top of the anvil. I want it to look like a human being touched it. I like the idea of shamanism. The blacksmith was, in ancient times, a magical figure. He could do things. I think very few contemporary people have the pleasure of finding out what that's about.

Rick: People don't understand the physical environment they live in. We get further and further away from it every day. And that has happened in only one or two generations.

Tom: It bothers me a lot as a teacher. I haven't mentioned much about that. I see students come in who don't even know what a screwdriver is. They don't know that a hammer will drive a nail. They've never tried it. I have to start from the beginning and tell people, "This is a drill press." They ask, "What does a drill press do?" And I say, "It drills holes"—things I learned as a farm kid in my grandfather's shop. Everybody knew what a drill press did back in those days because every-

René Magritte's Damascus Pig Confronts Swartz's Inverted Anvil

body had experience with tools, direct experience with the world around them.

Rick: Well, times certainly have changed for most people, especially in a high-tech urban culture where everything is done by machines or somebody else. One final question: Why did you continue with blacksmithing?

Tom: Rick, I've asked myself the same question, and I truly believe it was my own dogged determination. I wouldn't give up and I couldn't believe I had finally found something that I couldn't master easily, because I'm a quick study. I learned arc welding like it was nothing. I learned other fabricating techniques very quickly. I had watched blacksmiths work and it looked easy, so I tried it and thought, this is something I can spend ten years doing and get to the point where I realize that I don't know anything. And that's precisely what has happened to me now. Even though I call myself a blacksmith, I don't call myself someone who knows everything about blacksmithing. That would be foolish.

Blacksmithing is an expansive thing. The more you know about it, the more there is to know and that keeps my interest. I keep finding new things, new books, new ways of doing things. I enjoy the idea of having learned something and having decided that that's the way to do it and then having someone else show me how foolish I am for doing all those steps. I enjoy the surprise of saying, well, wrong again, and I like the fact that blacksmithing in this country is growing in a sense that perhaps no one anticipated. Certainly, the level of craftsmanship is amazing now compared to the really crude things that we saw and did even ten years ago. It's expanding in directions that few of us anticipated, certainly not me. So I just wanted the challenge. I wanted something that would keep me interested.

Rick: Maybe it's the immediacy of blacksmithing—having to make all those decisions quickly while the iron is cooling off.

Tom: Yes, I think so. There's so much in sculpture that's indirect. I've left out a big chunk of my career here. I was welding these steel sculptures that I used to make and then spray painting them with acrylic lacquers. I got incredibly beautiful finishes on them, just like plastic. Then I'd take them to a show and some jerk would scratch them, and I'd be heartbroken because I knew that I'd have to paint the whole thing over again. I said to myself, I can't keep this up. The stress of this is going to make me sick. I needed something that was more direct, more durable. I thought that blacksmithing, forged things, would serve that need, and indeed they have. You know that if you get a dent, you can reheat, blend the surface in. They're very easy to repair. They last forever inside, and I make sculpture that stays inside. I don't make outdoor sculpture. So there was another strong reason for me, the directness of blacksmithing. I realized something about my personality. I didn't like bronze casting as well as blacksmithing because I didn't like all the indirect work that didn't seem to be serving the purpose of the piece. I liked the idea of beating on the work and seeing a dent—immediately.

Another reason why I pressed in the direction of being a blacksmith other than the fact that I love doing it was because I knew if I was going to survive in the university business, I needed to have something people were interested in, and I determined early on that people enjoy watching blacksmiths work. I admit that this is very crass, but I

knew I had a commercial skill I could market. I had to survive. I'd gotten this job, and many people had applied for it. I discovered that it was one thing to get a job teaching at a university, but it was quite another to keep it because of all these people breathing down your neck who wanted the position. One way of getting tenure and promotions was to show my creative work, my sculpture, drawings, but another way was to do workshops and to get myself into a position where people would be interested in my work. It was sort of a planned thing, a game plan. I was merchandising my career.

Rick: Do you think blacksmithing does something for you personally on a psychological level when you're working?

Tom: Well, maybe, Rick. Perhaps the most important reason of all for staying in blacksmithing is that I get great pleasure out of beating the hell out of that metal. I think it's an emotional cathartic, a stress reliever that's better than drugs or alcohol or anything I can think of. We talked earlier about gratification. I make art for probably the same reasons I like to beat on metal. It makes me feel better. It makes me understand myself, and that's why I'm an artist in the first place.

Rick: I suppose there's a certain element of aggression and anger in all of us, you know, and blacksmithing is an acceptable, constructive way of dealing with it. I can come into the shop in some foul mood, and after concentrating for four or five hours on the metalwork, the mood lifts. I walk out of there and I'm tired, but my mind is clear and things have changed.

Tom: Personally, I think that getting rid of frustration and aggression is a universal need that isn't satisfied at the office and isn't satisfied generally in modern times.

I think that holistic is a very apt, very accurate descriptive term for the way I see my work. I never expected that the catalyst would be watching my grandfather work at the forge, but I've often wondered, to carry this a step further, who taught him? Somebody had to teach him. He was an accomplished blacksmith. He hardened and tempered. He forge welded. Somebody taught him and that keeps going back. I don't believe that I'm just stuck in space and that my work is so unique that nothing else exists. I believe that my work is part of a continuum. I love going to museums except that they spook me out because I hear voices. I hear voices with blacksmithing, too, like when I go to Europe and see an old forge shop. It'll unhinge you to go into a building where there's a forge that hasn't been lit for two hundred years. You know that there were men working there. You know what it would have been like to work in there. You could walk right in and work there now, light a fire in that forge, and make useful things. Well, artists have been making art since before there was a term for it. It has taken me a long time to realize that art is based on universal human values.

Roberta Ann Elliott-Francis

Roberta Ann Elliott-Francis *has been*
actively working as an artist blacksmith for about
seven years. She lives outside Cobden, Illinois, where
she has established her shop, The Velvet Hammer. She
was interviewed in the blacksmith shop at Southern
Illinois University, Carbondale.

Rick: Would you tell me about your early experiences
with blacksmithing?

Bert: Around 1978 I was trying to find someone to teach
me how to shoe horses. I thought anybody who
did blacksmithing also knew how to shoe horses,
so I ended up in a welding course out at STC
[SIU's School of Technical Careers]. Then here in
the art department at SIU, Brent [Kington; see part
5] was teaching a class, and I sat in on it for about
the first month or two of the semester. I got a feel
for how to get the fire started and what could be
done with metal, but I didn't do that much work
with metal. My other responsibilities took over.

Rick: What were they?

Bert: I was a graduate student in physiology, and research and other course work took priority.

Rick: So blacksmithing was an interest that you were de-
veloping while you were a graduate student here?

Bert: Yes. I knew I didn't want to continue in physiology as a profession, and I thought, well, what
better profession than horseshoeing. I needed
a change.

Rick: Did you complete your degree?

Bert: Yes. I got my Ph.D. in 1980. I went to horseshoeing school a month after I finished here, and that's really where I learned my hand control. We'd pound on iron or horses' feet for eight hours a day, five days a week, and I found out that I could do it, that I enjoyed doing it. At that point, I wasn't making much more than a horseshoe, but I was learning other skills.

Rick: Hammer control?

Bert: Hammer control, using other types of tools, that sort of thing—a different type of orientation.

Rick: Working the fire?

Bert: I learned a different way of working the fire and the metal than I had with Brent because you're working under different conditions. Out in the barn, you don't have all the facilities that you would in a shop. You have to learn to compensate. It made me look at processes in different ways, trying to find the best way at the time. That was a real learning experience, and had I never gone to horseshoeing school, I probably never would have gotten into blacksmithing. When I was there, I bought an anvil and a gas forge and tools.

I really didn't start working at blacksmithing until I got my shop in Makanda [Illinois] and set up strict hours for myself. And if I was going to be there, I was going to work. That was nice, the first time I had a place to do my work. Since I was unemployed and not shoeing horses, I could play—just experiment—and that's mainly how I've learned most of my skills, by the seat of my pants, experimenting and screwing up. I hate to throw anything away. It's got to have a use in some way. From a screw-up, I think, well, what can I do with

this to make it better?, and that's when I have my biggest growth spurts. Invariably, I find something new and different that the iron would do that I'd never tried or even thought about trying before. Right now I'm working with pipe, and that was just by a fluke that I started finding these different designs to forge from pipe.

When I was here [at the SIUC blacksmith shop] the first time, I knew so little I couldn't take advantage of it. Now when I see someone in the shop working, doing something that I've tried to do, I learn from them, whereas before I wouldn't have been able to do that because I didn't have the experience necessary. I just didn't know the value of what I was seeing.

Rick: You can't see the subtleties of the process if you don't know what's going on in the process.

Bert: The design, everything. And at first it was hard for me to be around any other blacksmiths. I had to be off on my own to gain self-confidence. When I was in the SIUC shop, I felt shy at first because I didn't know what to expect or how I would be accepted, but that quickly was put to rest. Now I think the qualities that I have going for me are ambition, perseverance, and self-confidence. I never questioned whether I'd be able to blacksmith. I don't think I've achieved that to the extent that I would like, but I don't question that I will. I do a lot of production work, and there's always the drive to do it the most efficient way. You always have to try a slightly different technique to see if that's faster, to get a better finished look. It's a matter of honing your techniques.

Rick: I know from my own experience that you're smart to do some production work. If you do custom work all the time, it takes more tooling. Every job

is a new problem, and every bid is a new problem. Production work is more predictable.

Bert: You can extrapolate.

Rick: Right, exactly. You have more control of your business in a sense. I've seen some of your work, coat racks and coat hangers and chandeliers. What are you working on now?

Bert: A candle chandelier. I'm still working on the design for an electrified one. It's sitting on the drawing board. I do what I call functional art. I do much better when I can start with a function and design from there. It's really hard for me just to do sculpture. I've done a few, like the flowers I'm doing with the pipe are sculptural, but I like making something that someone likes to use. It gives them pleasure to hold it, to use it, so that it means something to them. It becomes a part of them because they're using it. That's mainly what I go for. Under that category, there are innumerable things—fireplace sets, dinner bells, trivets to go by a fireplace or on wood stoves, hinges. I make numbers for doors and that sort of thing.

I also enjoy being aware of nature. That comes out in my work. I use that as a motif. I've become much more aware since I moved to this place in the woods about two years ago—the power of nature and also its sensitivity. The thing I've learned the most from is the creek. Most of the time, like right now, it's maybe six inches deep, and there are some pools where it's maybe two feet deep. After the rain, particularly after the flood we had recently, it was a hundred feet wide and it came up and pushed leaves against one of the foundation poles of the house.

Rick: How do you market your work?

Bert: I have one store in Carbondale that does very well with my stuff and gives me a lot of publicity. I've gotten a few custom orders because of them. The majority is by word of mouth or craft fairs.

Rick: You do go to craft fairs?

Bert: I'm slowly experimenting. I work about two fairs a year because I have this fear of being overwhelmed with too much to do. I feel that sort of pressure easily. I get very anxious when I get an order. I want it done next week. But if I get fifteen orders, it's impossible to get them all done next week. It's just a pressure I put on myself. I don't want to produce something that's going to hang around for three years. I've done enough of those. I don't want to rely on fairs, however. I don't like to travel that much, and they're very time consuming.

Rick: You've got to have somebody with you to give you breaks, too, don't you?

Bert: I do the one out at Logan [John A. Logan College, Carterville, Illinois] by myself just because I know I'll have friends coming through and they'll give me a breather for fifteen or twenty minutes, but that's not possible anyplace else. The other thing is that 50 percent of my profit is from custom orders I obtain at the fair, so I have to be there. Fairs are good for exposure and if you don't do too many, they can be fun. One a month would be fine. You're meeting interesting people and you slowly develop friends, the other craftspeople you start seeing at repeat fairs. I've only been doing it for probably a year and a half, so I'm a newcomer. I'm meeting these people who are old buddies from way back when. There's a lot to learn from their experiences—just how to deal with fairs, what the crowds like, what their price limit is, and that sort of thing.

Rick: What are the reactions of people to a woman blacksmith?

Bert: I've never felt any discrimination from another blacksmith. I just assume they see my work and they say, "Okay, she's a blacksmith." But there's always the look of astonishment, "Oh, you did this." Like when I go to fairs and they see my business card and it says "Bert" on it, they just naturally assume it's a man. It usually makes them take a second look. My favorite story is about a man who came down to my shop in Makanda. He said, "How long you been a lady blacksmith?" I told him, "I've been a lady for thirty something years, and I've been a blacksmith for about five years." It doesn't bother me in the least when they're surprised because I recognize that I'm definitely in a minority. I'm even taken aback when I meet another woman blacksmith.

Rick: You got your Ph.D. in physiology. Why would you want to do blacksmithing after making that intense effort to get a Ph.D.?

Bert: I'd been around horses for a long time. I never owned them but I'd ridden them a lot, and I always liked pounding on things, making hammer marks in my piano bench, and so on. I like physical exertion and the feeling it gives me. And yet your brain doesn't go to sleep when you're smithing because you have to think. One of the hardest things for me is dealing with three dimensions in my head. I think I've learned so much that way, teaching myself. It's much more satisfying than all the physiology I ever learned, even though I think that subject matter is fascinating. But for me, there was just no future in it.

Anyway, I wanted to stay in this area, so I needed to find something to support myself. I did   **Roses**

want to be self-employed. I've always been a loner, and I don't work that well with other people—just to a limited extent. I like to work at my own pace, and generally that's a little faster than most people I know. I like to work at a steady pace. When I get tired, okay I'll quit then. I set goals and when I reach a goal, I'll take a break. But you can only do that when you're self-employed. I set my own hours and they're somewhat flexible, so that's nice.

I also like being strong. I like being able to do a lot for myself, and I have a pretty good idea of what my limits are—I think I've explored them enough. Now I'm at the peak of how much I'd like to exert myself.

Rick: It's pretty obvious that no matter how physically strong you are, that's not going to get it in iron-working anyway. If you're going to do any heavy forging, everybody uses a power hammer or a striker. I think it's your ability to pick up on instant changes in the material that's crucial.

Bert: Anyway, I don't know if I really have an answer to your question about why I became a blacksmith. If something presents itself and it seems like the right time, I say, "Okay." Much of my life has been that way—I can think of only one or two exceptions that haven't turned out very well. And blacksmithing seemed like the thing to do, like someone just took me by the hand and said, "Let's go this way."